# SECRET FORDS

## 70s AND 80s RS ICONS EDITION

### COMPANION BOOK TO SECRET FORDS VOLUME ONE

7S
SEVEN SPOKE PUBLISHING

## By the same author

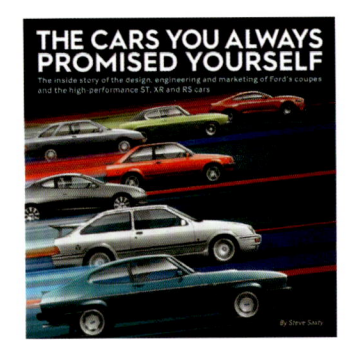

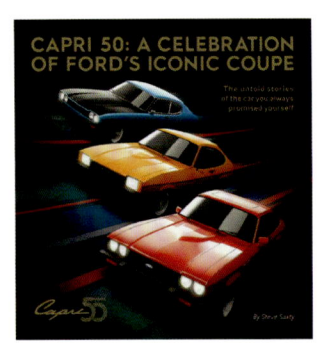

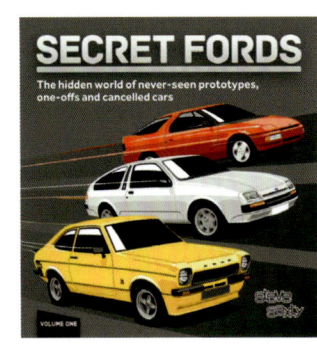

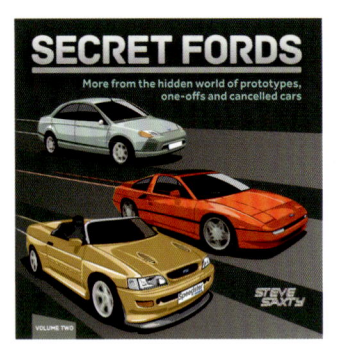

**Copyright Steve Saxty 2022**

All rights reserved. No part of this publication may be reproduced, stored in a retrieval system or transmitted, in any form or by any means, electronic, mechanical, photocopying, recording or otherwise, without prior permission in writing from the publisher.

First published in April 2022

978-1-8382232-5-0 (Secret Fords Volume 1 RS Icons Companion Book)
978-1-8382232-6-7 (Secret Fords Vol 1 RS Icons Limited Edition Two-book Set)

Published by
Seven Spoke Publishing
Tel: +44 20 8133 9276
www.stevesaxty.com

Design & Layout by Adrian Morris
Edited by Mel Nichols
Printed by Gomer Press Ltd

### COPYRIGHT

We have made every effort to trace and acknowledge copyright holders and we apologise in advance for any unintentional omission. We would be pleased to insert the appropriate acknowledgement in any subsequent edition.

# THE HIDDEN GEMS OF RS

Ford has so many iconic treasures in its back catalogue. The mere mention of names like Capri, Sierra, Escort and, of course, the RS cars, brings a smile to any enthusiast's face. That was the idea behind this book – to delight you with more unseen pictures that bring these cars to life, starting at their birth. After writing the two *Secret Fords* editions – and experiencing the delight of seeing *Volume One* sell out in a year – I knew exactly what readers enjoyed. The biggest hit of the series has been the *RS Special Collector's Edition* multi-book set of *Volume Two*.

Combining that insight with the first volume quickly selling out, I was prompted to bring it back in the same vein as a two-book set, the *RS Special Icons Edition* which includes this book you're holding, the new companion to *Secret Fords Volume One*. It's not a substitute for its 304-page big brother but is, I think, a perfect RS-led, visually driven complement that I hope will surprise and delight.

It incorporates the original content of – and, because it is almost five times larger, substantially builds on – the Scrapbook that was part of the earlier *Volume One Collector's Edition*. This new companion book has been a joy to create. Allow me a moment to say why. First, it's a way of celebrating these iconic Fords by being able to reproduce a number of the unseen photos of them in an expansive two-page format. I had so much to write in the main *Secret Fords* books that we didn't always get the chance to let the images speak as loudly as the words.

Second, it is my opportunity to share with you a mass of fascinating material that's poured in since I wrote *Secret Fords Volume One*. I kept getting more help, more info and more jaw-dropping photos, especially of the RS cars, from the people who created them. Nearly every image on the pages ahead has sat unseen for decades. This book sets them free. So many people entrusted them to me with love and care that they deserved more than a minute's Facebook fame. It's right that they should be enjoyed in print.

The RS legend and the Ford design story are interwoven. That's why each volume of *Secret Fords* tells the tale of the main cars – Fiesta, Escort, Capri, Sierra, etc – alongside their relatively spicy RS versions. In my view, it's the only way to understand how the cars you love now, or did back then, came to be. This companion book is also a chance for me to write a little more personally by dipping out of the near-silent role of your narrator. The result is, I hope, a different – and occasionally more intimate – take on the journey through the '70s and '80s. I must confess that I took great delight in unearthing the origins of the RS brand – we *all* know what the two letters stand for, but I had no idea where they came from. For the first time, we discover how Rallye Sport actually started. The shadows of Escort, and especially Sierra and Capri, loom over Ford's most iconic '70s and '80s cars and, since I fear it will be many years – if ever – until I revisit the heroes I loved, then this book is also a fond farewell.

steve s3xty

### Escort RS2000 Signal Yellow
In the mid '70s new paint technology allowed stronger, more vibrant colours. Ford cannily marketed these as 'Signal' paints in red, green, amber, yellow, orange and red.

### Capri *turbo* Strato Silver
The wide-arched Capri is one of the rarest RS models. Silver was chosen as the launch colour because it showed off the flared bodywork far better than Ford Motorsport's traditional white.

### Sierra RS Cosworth Crystal Blue
The second-generation Cosworth could be had in more sophisticated colours than the original three-door, such as Ford's new 'Crystal' metallic finishes. This denim-hued Crystal Blue granted the RS family man a little more stealth.

### RS1700T Diamond White
Ford Motorsport made 11 prototype RS1700Ts — nine in white plus one in Caspian Blue and one in Cardinal Red. White allowed easy inspection of a prototype for body damage, and easy repair.

### Sierra RS Cosworth Rosso Red
The three-door Sierra Cosworths were painted either Black, Diamond White or Moonstone Blue. Except this one, which was created for the Duke of Bedford and painted red on the line in Genk but instead ended up as a test car for Ford's SVE group.

### RS200 Diamond White
White was Ford's primary motorsport colour until the 2000s. All the RS200s were manufactured in Diamond White. However, Tickford repainted six cars red, mid-blue and black before delivery.

### Capri RS2600 Le Mans Green
The vivid '70s were all about Day-Glo 'safety' colours that swept away dingy greens, reds and whites. Appropriately, Ford labelled its loud new paints after roaring racetracks with names like Sebring Red and Daytona Yellow.

RS ICONS EDITION **005**

# WIND TUNNEL MODELS

Until 1983, when Ford opened its wind tunnel, future cars were tested using one-fifth or one-third scale models. They hardly looked glamorous in their unpainted black 'epowood' finish, but this selection was painted a rainbow of colours and kept locked away at the Merkenich design studio. In 2017, they were passed to the Cologne museum where these shots were taken. I managed to squeeze a few into *Secret Fords Volume One* but there are many more, so here's a longer look. If you do the factory tour, you'll get to see the museum. Make sure to ask nicely; see if you can peer at the models as they sleep peacefully in their crates.

**Treasure chests**
I found about 30 models buried in these unopened wooden crates at Ford. I managed to get the Taunus/Cortina outside but this poor Granada Mark II didn't make it.

**RS ICONS EDITION 007**

### Five-door Cosworth

A five-door Sierra Cosworth was never considered for production so why make this model of it, faithful in every way except for the number of side apertures? There's a simple explanation. The full-sized car was tested for key aero points such as rear wing location, which determined required downforce. It's likely that this giant one-third-scale model was laying around and surplus to requirements. The obvious thing to do was to remodel it for initial wind tunnel testing only where it counted, so it did not matter how many door handles were on the side. Thus, the smallest Cosworth was born. The wheels may look like the real thing but no; they are just pieces of paper.

008  Secret Fords

**Last of the line**
There are about 12 of these models in Ford's Cologne museum. The youngest, just a mere 40 years old, is the Prairie Yellow Taunus/Cortina. The eagle-eyed will spot that it is the facelifted '80 model – Project Teresa – a stop-gap car intended to fill in for the Sierra that started late after its predecessor, Project Linda, was cancelled. Why no more scale models after that? Well, the miniature bloodline faded away when the new wind tunnel in Merkenich meant that Ford's designers and engineers could move to full-sized models. However, the quarter-scale model had a final fling later in the '80s.
To keep costs down the designers experimented with them as a way of evaluating new designs against each other.

RS ICONS EDITION  **009**

### Spoiled for choice
It took two men to lift this giant one-third scale Sierra model from its crated slumber. To our delight, we found a set of spoilers rattling around underneath. Then we realised what this model had been used for. The Sierra launched with questions about its crosswind stability. It was hastily fixed by adding rubber 'ears' around the rear windows to upset the airflow and reduce lift. These were earlier, less elegant experimental solutions — sticking spoilers all over the Sierra. A full-sized RS Owners Club chairman gives a good indication of scale.

### A matter of scale
But something strange happened when quarter scale models were used for appraising first-look designs. The problem is that the human eye reads a smaller scale model differently from the real thing, which is three or four times bigger. The quarter-scale car models lost their personality and there was much discussion about why nobody liked using them. The realisation was that the human eye looks at detail to help differentiate. To see for yourself, observe model figures such as a child's doll or toy soldier and you'll see that many of their faces look the same. It's also true of a vehicle. Until the full-sized design is finished there's little point making a smaller-scale model for visual evaluation. That's why, even in an age where it is possible to make a vehicle without a clay model, it is still standard practice to make a full-sized item before any metal-bashing commences.

## Coupe line-up
The XR4 still fascinates me. It was such a strong design but too far ahead of its time and too soft to drive. The two Capris alongside belong to an earlier era. They tugged at my heartstrings more back in the day, and I wasn't alone. When you see the XR4 alongside the RS2800 and the regular Capri II, the difference between the two coupes could not be starker. I couldn't include these shots in the main book, which covers each car in date order. But they look fine sitting together – a miniature classic car show of Ford prototypes.

## Nose job
The XR4 wind tunnel model is fascinating for its detail. Look at the carefully sculpted bodykit, which is faithful in every way. The nose shows a join line where different front ends could be put on and taken off to be tested until reaching this final design.

RS ICONS EDITION  **011**

**Rainbow warriors**
It's hard not to feel like a kid when you have this lot to play with. They might look equally cute, but the models are quite different. The red and blue Escorts are carved from heavy 'epowood' that makes them extraordinarily heavy, while later models like the Sierra are made of glassfibre. This group hadn't seen daylight in decades and may never be set out together like this again.

**Two little old ladies**
The original Escort and the later Mark II Brenda were before my time, so they never played a role in my life. But as I researched Secret Fords, I came to realise how important they were and what a difficult job Brenda had as the follow-up to the first model. These two Escorts, the oldest two in any form in the world, certainly deserve a place in history. You might wonder why there isn't such an exquisitely carved Mark III in the collection. It's because one sheepish former employee, who confessed to me, has kept it in his loft!

# ORIGINS OF THE RALLYE SPORT BRAND

Every Ford enthusiast knows RS stands for Rallye Sport, complete with a German-style 'e' on the end of Rally but nobody seemed to know how the brand name started. This set me off on a quest to figure out how the two letters became synonymous with Ford's highest-performing cars, long before Porsche decided to use them. I'd driven more RS cars than I could count and yet I had no idea how the brand started until I exchanged emails with Wolfgang Wagner and Thilo Moerke at the Ford Oldtimer und Motorsport Club in Cologne.

The tale starts in spring '67 when Ford of Germany heard rumours that Opel, its GM nemesis, was about to launch sporty versions of its family cars as the Kadett Rallye and Rekord Sprint. Ford was using the TS name – *Tourensport* – for its sporty models and decided it needed a response to Opel's new Rallye and Sprint duo that sounded more urgent than the leisurely Touring Sport. Easy: swap in the word Opel was using – Rallye. So Ford replaced TS with RS and the two Rallye Sport cars were conceived in just a few months, ahead of the autumn 1967 Frankfurt Show.

Ford of Germany had called its saloon cars Taunus since the '50s; the front-wheel drive Taunus 12M was similar in appeal to the British Cortina while the bigger RWD 17M and 20M tackled the larger end of the market. Calling two different cars with the same Taunus name confused everyone, so when they were replaced in the late '60s the Taunus name was dropped and they became the Ford 12M/15M (P6) and the Ford 17M/20M/26M (P7) respectively. To turn these two – a mid-sized German FWD family car and an executive machine – into the first RS cars in time for the September '67 Frankfurt show required some fast thinking. Their credibility rested on more power and sportier looks inside and out, a template for the decades to follow.

The smaller 15M RS was unveiled at the Frankfurt Show as a coupe and the 20M RS as a two-door, although both could be purchased as a coupe and two- or four-door saloon. The 15M RS was powered by a 1.7litre V4 engine producing 70bhp for a top speed just under 100mph. It went on sale in March '68, along with a 17M RS derivative which swapped in the 2.0litre Cologne V6 that developed 90bhp. They were billed as 'two genuine rally cars'. The larger 20M RS was equipped with a 2.3litre V6 and, with a top speed of 104mph (167km/h), was the fastest car in Ford of Germany's portfolio. The official Ford press release charmingly announced: "One of the specialities of the Rallye Sports versions are their functional and well-equipped cockpits. The instrument panels have two circular dials – rev counter and speedometer – so as to always hit the driver's eye" and "both models feature a short floor shift stick". Without any trace of irony it proclaimed: "Rounding up the picture of a pure-bred rally sports car are simulated-wood steering wheel and gear shift knob." Although RS grew out of a need to spoil the debut of two long-forgotten Opels, Ford's RS brand took the lead as it began to earn its sporting credentials on road and track.

**The first two RS models**
The 'K-LN-000' plates denote that these were most likely the sign-off design cars for the RS 20M and 15M. Production versions included sporty chrome wheel trims. This photo is the birth of RS.

RS ICONS EDITION  **013**

**The FWD RS Coupe**
The red P6-generation (Project 6) 15M RS was the raciest of the mid-sized FWD German Fords in this coupe form. The 15M was sold mainly as a four-door and a two-door but this coupe — its name literally means 'cut' in French — used a cut-down rear window to give it a rakish, sporty look. The RS versions were available in each of the three body styles, garnished with a vinyl roof, 'Rallye' side stripes, halogen fog lamps, chrome sporty steel rims and grille. The RS interior featured three spoke sports steering wheel, optional Recaro seats, standard floor shifter, rev counter, ammeter, and oil pressure gauge.

**RS crosses the chequered flag**
The first competitive outing for a works RS car was this 20M RS entered in the '68 London-Sydney Marathon with legendary Belgian rally driver Gilbert Staepelaere at the wheel. It finished 16th, not bad for a large executive coupe – RS's winning ways were just around the corner. This photo celebrates the first win for an RS, the 1969 Safari Rally, with honours taken by Robin Hillyar.

RS ICONS EDITION  **015**

### Large RWD RS Coupe
The 17M RS coupe (with the 2.0litre V6) that resides in Ford's Cologne museum is a so-called P7b model, that was facelifted only a year after the launch of the unsuccessful 17M/20M P7a. The P7b RS models tidied up the looks of the earlier 20M RS. Deleting the bonnet scoops and other details gave it a sleeker look until it eventually handed over to the Granada. The smaller 15M would eventually be replaced in 1970 when the Taunus name was wisely reinstated.

### LHD only?
The RS brand was always closest to the hearts of British enthusiasts. Some LHD markets were less enthusiastic, even choosing to delete the two letters on their versions. So it is understandable that British enthusiasts might assume that the later AVO Escorts were the first of the breed, or that these first two German RS cars were LHD only. Not so; Ford in South Africa also made the 20M RS in RHD.

016    Secret Fords

*Courtesy Steve Aylen*

# JET: THE FASTEST-LOOKING CAPRI

When I first saw these photos of the Capri JET I was astonished. OK, so look closely and you see that the front wheels sit on spindles, just like a model Capri — well, it *was* a model... just a full-sized one. We had to squeeze it onto a single page in *Secret Fords Volume One*, resulting in many of the wonderful tiny details being almost impossible to spot. So let's take a look now at what Ford's designers were doing back in September '68, a few months before the production car was shown to the world.

It's easy to get lost, or at least bewildered, by the gas turbine connotations of the rear that back up the JET name but let's probe a little deeper. This Capri has no interior and was probably a fibreglass model, quite possibly the final one used to sign off the car. It certainly explains how the indentation with the F O R D letters sits so neatly in the bonnet and the front end is flushed in to remove the mounting points where the bumpers sat. The dummy air scoops that helped define the original Capri are made to look functional and, thanks to some clever stripe-work, seem to scream off from the front like... er, a jet. Then there is the window blackout treatment, years before such things became fashionable in the '70s, that extends around the A-post to add a visor-like visage of sophistication missing in the raunchy production Capri. Note, too, the race-style door mirrors, wheels and bonnet vents — changes that gave this car a makeover like none other. Make no bones about it: whoever did this one-off Capri might have been having fun but knew what they were doing.

# WHEN 4X4 WAS A STEP TOO FAR

The idea for an all-wheel drive Capri — or 4x4, as the technology used to be called in the old days — has its genesis in farmyard 4x4 vehicles. So it's no wonder that this prototype AWD Capri is at home tearing across the rutted mud surrounding the fields of Ford's Boreham facility where the Competitions Department was based.

At the 4x4's heart lay the work of Harry Ferguson who was born into a farming family but made his fame and fortune thanks to a fascination with machines. After becoming the first Irishman to make and fly an aircraft, he moved on to setting up the successful Ferguson tractor company with two partners, one of them being David Brown, later of Aston DB fame. Ferguson's tractors used a novel linkage that made them stable. Later, Harry set off on a lifelong quest to add stability to road cars. He set up Harry Ferguson Research and an offshoot called FF that took over selling the Ferguson Formula technology that included advanced features like AWD and anti-lock brakes.

The British Ministry of Technology thought the idea had merit and sponsored the Home Office Police Scientific Development Branch (no doubt un-snappily called HOPSDM) to evaluate 22 police-spec Ford Zodiacs converted by HFR to AWD in 1968.

Police drivers preferred the large Ford's automatic transmission and the Essex 3.0litre V6 so that's what they got, along with exotic-for-the time Dunlop Maxaret anti-lock brakes.

The Zodiac police cars were delivered in the months before the Capri was launched in January '69 and so preproduction Capris were available to the Competitions Department, led by Henry Taylor, who had two 1600GTs sent to HFR. Harry's technicians stuffed in the Zodiac's V6 with auto transmission and Ferguson Formula's AWD, then returned the pair to Boreham, where the Ford engineers promptly fitted race-spec Weslake heads to deliver 160bhp in January '69. Just days after the production Capri was announced, rally hero and Ford works driver Roger Clark raced the car at Croft where – against all odds – he won all three races. The first Capri racer was joined by another two, possibly three, AWD Capri siblings.

All was looking good for the AWD Capri in 1969. But a year later the tide had turned. Roger Clark's car, alongside another campaigned by his brother Stan, and another by Rod Chapman, was upgraded with aluminium cylinder heads and fuel injection to deliver 252bhp, transmitted through a five-speed gearbox. But in the '70/71 season they failed to deliver on the early promise shown by Roger's car in that first televised race.

**Preproduction Capri goes 4x4**
This was the first 3.0litre Capri, up and running even before the normal car had been announced. Harry Ferguson Research (HFR) converted a preproduction 1600GT road car to Essex 3.0litre power in late '68 by using the same auto gearbox and engine that was fitted to 22 police-spec Ford Zodiacs. Here, in the hands of rally legend Roger Clark, it launches itself out of a snowy rut in the fields around Boreham, the windswept former aerodrome where the Competitions Department was based. A year later, Roger's car was upgraded with fuel injection that deployed six giant air-sucking trumpets sprouting through the bonnet (left).

At the same time, Advanced Vehicle Operations — which handled production of cars with a competition bent — was serious about the AWD Capri. It even installed AWD rolling road testing equipment after another three road-going FF Capris were made and demonstrated to the press, who loved them. But AVO was also developing the mighty RS2600 for circuit racing. This was a far greater and more glamorous arena — hurtling around Spa was undoubtedly more in keeping with the Capri's target aspirations than to be seen plugging around in British mud.

Because Ford could sell every RWD coupe it could make, the AWD Capri was becoming redundant. Rod Mansfield, the legendary engineer behind so many of the iconic fast Fords, recalls the issue. "The AWD kit was really a tight fit in the small Capri and making a production version would have been far too disruptive for the factory," he says. "We could justify special lightweight RS2600s because they could be made in batches and then the later regular versions came down the line because the RS2600 wasn't difficult for the factory to handle. But the AWD installation would have required so much off-line reworking that it would have been impractical to make in any volume." The RS2600 and RS3100 were simply better as RS road cars and even better for building the overall reputation of the RWD Capri. All-wheel drive would feature in many of the RS cars that followed, but not this one.

RS ICONS EDITION  **021**

### Capri approaches for take-off
Although it bears the same 73 decal as Roger Clark's Capri on the previous page, this car is probably the other of the first two preproduction 1600GTs cars converted by HFR to AWD. It's certainly seen some competition use but the black vinyl roof is testament to it being a converted road car. Here, in the hands of Ford works rally driver Ove Andersson, it seems to tear at the road as it launches forward. The skyward-facing nose, like an aircraft taking off, was a style beloved of Ford Design boss, American Joe Oros, that few European designers understood at the time. Maybe they needed to see this photo!

# GT70 PHOTO SHOOT

Today's studio shoots are little different from those of decades past. A car, shot against a neutral backdrop, and lots of trial-and-error frames. Well... not everything is the same: back in 1971 car makers started using fashion photographers to photograph cars. Hardly any images from this strip were ever used – they were instantly dated by the fashion. It's a shame. Look past the bizarre costumes and it's easy to see that the cameraman went to some lengths to capture the car from novel angles. This is the fifth GT70, rebodied in Turin by the Ford studio that would duly merge with Ghia. It was a breathtaking car but a non-runner and, when the regular GT70 was cancelled, few records remained of it. That was until the Ford archivists discovered these in 2020 while helping me research the *Secret Fords* books. The clothes may be dated but the car has a timeless appeal.

RS ICONS EDITION  023

## History Repeats itself

The full story of this delightful one-off GT70 is told in full in *Secret Fords Volume One* so there is no need to repeat it in depth here. The other four GT70s were pretty, Lotus-like wannabees but that wasn't enough for design boss Joe Oros who commissioned Ghia's team to style this car as a design exercise. Two decades later, in the mid '90s, Escort RS2000 designer Tom Scott wanted to do the same and stretch Ford design. He had moved on to head up Advanced Design in Detroit and his team created their vision for a futuristic road racing sports car. Naturally they selected a number in the series from GT40 to GT70 and so the new car became the GT90. Although it wasn't intended for production, it caused such a stir that there were a few speculative discussions about making a version of it. They came to nothing but the idea didn't die. During the height of the 2000s retrofuturism fad typified by the New Beetle and Mini, the son-of-GT90 supercar idea morphed into the reborn GT40, simply called GT because of a naming copyright issue with the old GT40 name. GT70 was stillborn but left a contemporary legacy nonetheless.

RS ICONS EDITION  025

## DESIRABLE SECRET RS

It's inevitable that I've been asked which of the secret Fords should have been made. As Richard Parry-Jones explained in the intro to the main *Secret Fords Volume One* book, sometimes it's just a question of timing. So here's my view: if the time had been right then Ford should have made the Capri RS2800. But the 1974/75 Oil Crisis was not the right time and Richard's point is vindicated. Even so, I still wish the RS2800 — and enthusiasts — had been a little luckier. I love telling the tale of the RS2800 but never quite seem to find the space to share all the photos. So here are a few more to enjoy. If there's one RS that never made it that I'd like to own, then this is it.

### Hiding in plain sight
I've seen this a few times and thought "That's a pretty sketch of the 'JPS Capri'" and moved on. But I — and many others — missed a trick. Look closely and the RS2800's front and rear spoilers are there. This is none other than the narrow-bodied iteration of the car on the next page. It only took me 30 years to spot this. Then, by chance I spied this yellow rendering by Karl-Heinz Nottrodt in a larger collection I saw online in the Car Design Archives, and now we have two RS2800 design sketches.

### Walkinshaw's one-off works RS2800
Tom Walkinshaw became famous as the owner of TWR, a 1500-strong company that ran everything from Rovers to Jaguars and BMWs in motorsport as well as handling road car design and development. TWR partnered with Jaguar on its JaguarSport cars, set up Holden Special Vehicles with GM in Australia and — thanks to designer Ian Callum — created the Aston Martin DB7 and Puma for Ford. Tom's initial career as a top-flight racer was founded during '74 when Ford contracted him to drive a Capri in the British Touring Car Championship. The next-gen Capri RS was intended to replace the heavy 3.0litre Essex V6 with a 2.8litre version of the engine from the RS2600. This is the first mule, pictured outside the offices of Ford's Boreham Motorsport department. The flared arches and spoilers are in place; all it needed was for the designers to tidy it up and hope the fuel crisis of the time wasn't going to deal a fatal blow.

*Courtesy Car Design Archives*

RS ICONS EDITION  **027**

**Wide-arched mystery no more**
The collection of wind tunnel models at the start of this book are tiny time capsules of work-in-progress. We all know the Capri RS2800 never came to pass but this model is a fantastic three-dimensional survivor that records what it might have been. From an on-high angle it looks like the real thing, ready to scream off — but it's just three feet long and its only motive power would be a hefty shove. Notice the Capri RS3100-inspired ducktail spoiler and running boards that neatly tie the front and rear arches together. This RS-that-nearly-was exudes a swagger that eludes the tamer-looking regular Capri II.

# RS2800 OUT ON THE ROAD

Ford has a long track record of letting journalists loose in prototypes to obtain their off – and sometimes on – the record opinions. The RS2800 was one such car that slipped out and into print, but not that many European car enthusiasts would have known. The American magazine *Road & Track* was given the honour of testing what eventually became a 95 per cent production-ready car. This is that car, a fantastic combination of every luxury and go-faster part that could be crammed into it:

- 165bhp engine: 2.8litre US-spec engine block, big-valve heads, high-lift cam, free-flow exhaust and electronic ignition
- Ghia interior: with unique RS Scheel seats front and rear, Blaupunkt stereo, RS steering wheel
- Exterior: US-spec 'Capri Midnight' body with 2.8 badging
- Chassis: RS3100 springs, dampers, and vented disc brakes, uprated rear pads.

**Final photos (opposite page)**
And for years that was the end of the story, or so I thought. The only photos of this unicorn survived in an old American car magazine. That was until 2019 when I spoke to RS2600 owner Michael Webster who showed me these photos. Sure enough: it was the same car, registered K-UR 744 but shorn of its gold wheels and stripery. Instead, it now bulged with the flared arches intended for it along, and four oversized round headlights glared out at me from the pictures. The RS2800 came so close but the photographic records of it were spread wide and far. But here they are finally together once and for all.

RS ICONS EDITION  029

*Courtesy Michael Webster*

## RAIDERS OF THE LOST ARCHIVES

This picture is just one hidden gem from the 30-plus photos I gathered of the design models created for the RS2000 and Mexico/RS1800. They are, I think, some of the rarest photos in this book and *Secret Fords Volume One*. There is an interesting story behind how they came to be here. Once I started writing, I discovered that a few black and white pictures of the RS2000 being designed had been published 20 years ago in *Rallye News*, the magazine of the RS Owners Club. I then found that a small set of them had been sold recently on eBay and the new owner, understandably, was unwilling to share them. Then someone kindly offered me a second set. They were reproductions – good but not quite good enough for a book.

I spoke to retired Ford designer Al Thorley. He thought he might have some prints in his loft – and was pretty sure these lost 40-year-old photos were colour! He kindly scanned the red and white Mexico shots. Then Al spoke to his friend Steve Aylen, who had another huge trove of the black and whites. Suddenly I had more than I needed of these never-seen photos, so let me share more here.

**The first RS2000 takes shape**
This is the original RS2000 model – notice the many tiny changes from the production car that followed. Look closely and there's a make-believe dashboard unlike any seen in an Escort and the exhaust is nothing more than a piece of pipe that's been sliced off at a jaunty angle.

**The genius of a good script**
The RS2000 logo – especially the entwined two-letter RS script – is much-loved by enthusiasts. Designer Tom Scott created it for the RS2000 first and then the Mexico. When the RS1800 was added in as a special-engined Mexico, then a third iteration was born. This is the hand-drawn piece of card that sat on the front and was then traced onto drawing paper to enable dies to be made for stamping out adhesive decals.

RS ICONS EDITION  031

*Courtesy Steve Aylen*

# THE BEAK-NOSED WONDER TAKES SHAPE

These two front ends show the progression of the RS2000 nose as designer Tom Scott inched towards the final design. The one on the left – as seen on the cover of this book – was a novel treatment but subject to stone-chipping at a time when paints and plastics lacked the flexibility of today's items. Tom moved forward to the design on the right, which we eventually saw in production. Note the lopsided wheelarches – one side with flares to cover 7-inch wheels and the other the more modest width seen in production. Having different sides, left and right, was a common technique for modelling cars back in the day. It was an easy way to compare alternatives. Today's designers can render their visions so perfectly that it is easier to create comparisons on-screen. But full-size models are still made, transferred from screen to clay by a three-axis mill in just days.

Many of the old Ford designers at Dunton remember Tom Scott's work on the RS2000. But nobody knew where he ended up after he moved to Jeep in the US. That wasn't good enough for his former boss Patrick le Quément: he started a global email hunt for Tom.

*Courtesy Steve Aylen*

Finally, Jack Telnack, Ford's former global design chief, told us he knew where Tom lived in Detroit. He had returned to Ford and risen through the ranks of Ford stateside. Within a day I was on the phone to Tom to get the RS2000's design story. Writing the *Secret Fords* books often connected me within hours to people. Finding these photos of the RS Escort and locating the man who designed it was an astonishing reminder of social media's power and email's reach. They can help authors locate sources and write richer stories in a way that would have been impossible 15 years ago.

**The plastic Escort**
This looks like a real Escort but it's merely a full-sized model restyled in clay. Its designer Tom Scott thinks that it was likely a fiberglass 'glazed shell' that was originally used to sign-off the three-door Escort. In the absence of real metal bodies being available, it was normal practice to reuse the fiberglass models that Design had laying around — it's still done today. So as convincing as this car looks, there is hardly a metal component in sight.

**Red equals Mexico, blue equals...**
The side view of Tom Scott's two models for the Escort RS2000 and Mexico show what might have been. The 1.6litre Mexico was added late to the programme, partly to add a flat front that the rally boys preferred, but mainly to add volume. Buyers were always confused that one could buy the almost identical-in-concept Escort 1600S, which left the pricier second-generation Mexico as something of an orphan. But things might have turned out differently if it had looked like this white car, emboldened with wide wheels and red decals. Instead, the production car lacked the flared arches mooted for it and retained the stripe kit from the regular 1600S with just the MEXICO decal for differentiation. Tom had a plan: he wanted the Mexico to have these fiery Mexican-red side stripes while its oh-so-British Cosworth BDA-powered RS1800 sister had two-tone blue stripes. Sadly, the bean counters had their way and so the Mexico lost its red flashes and faded from memory.

RS ICONS EDITION  **035**

*Courtesy Steve Aylen*

## FIRST RS FIESTA FINDS ITS FEET

The production Fiesta RS only existed in the '90s and is a car *Secret Fords Volume Two* readers will be familiar with. If I ever get around to *Volume Three* there's another cancelled Fiesta RS from the early 2000s to pick over. But this is grandad RS Fiesta, the Motorsport-developed proposal of the '70s. Three cars seem to have been made. The final silver one, registered K-PK 409, was given away as a prize after succeeding an earlier silver car registered, K-CC 572; and this white car, K-DY 510, which was the first. It has a retrimmed Fiesta S interior, black arches, and a tiny Motorsport sticker on the rear. It's a simple, low-cost way to make a sportier Fiesta.

RS ICONS EDITION **037**

### The ultimate Fiesta interior
The interior of this book's rear cover car was a fabulous mix of every possible Ghia, RS, and aftermarket accessory part – and that's where the problem started. The 1.1litre engine, spiced up with twin carbs, had little more zip than a 1.3litre. Add in that heavy and expensive interior and it's likely to have accelerated no faster than a regular 1100S. That's the eternal problem with small luxurious and affordable sporty cars – the greater the cost and weight added, the smaller the sales potential. Lovely to look at but not the right idea, this RS Fiesta was going nowhere. When the XR2 came along a few years later the Special Vehicle Engineering team and Ford's designers nailed it. They kept costs down by ditching all the fancy interior bits and the twin carbs in favour of more power from a larger, but mechanically simple, engine. The old Escort 'Simple Is Efficient' tagline summed up Ford at its best.

### Brothers in concept but not under the bonnet
This unusual composite of two shots shows the engine of the second Fiesta RS – K-CC 572 – alongside the works Fiesta driven by Ari Vatanen and navigator Dave Richards – yes *that* Dave Richards of Prodrive fame. The tuned-up 1600cc rally car was more highly strung than the twin-carb 1100cc unit fitted to this prototype road car alongside it. The Cologne-built Vatanen car shared the same blue stripe kit as the final silver RS car – and a shared destiny. Vatanen and Richards competed in the '79 Monte Carlo rally along with Roger Clark in a similar-spec Boreham-built Fiesta. They finished 10th and 13th respectively – a fair showing for a new competition car but Ford was used to winning and Clark was no fan. The 1600cc Fiesta rally car hadn't got off to the brightest start and the fortunes of its duller 1100cc road sibling duly dimmed accordingly and flickered out.

038    Secret Fords

# THE ALL-IN-ONE ESCORT CAPRI RS

Codenamed Erika, the new FWD '81 Escort was following on the heels of the new Fiesta during '79/80. This huge global project spawned two versions for Europe and North America, along with myriad unseen one-off concepts like these.

### Best left to rest
The Ghia files clearly label this car as 'Erika Capri RS' but it's really neither Capri nor RS and the name was probably just used to sell in the idea. Car designers and, to an extent, product planners, are some of the best salespeople in the business. To use the black and gold colour scheme of the old JPS Capri was genius but the execution of this Erika less so. There's no way it could ever be taken for a coupe.

```
Erika Scirocco 2-Passenger Rumbleseat              WB    94.6
Erika Program                                      OAL  156.3
Car No. 110W541                                    OAW   63.4
September 21, 1977                                 OAH   49

Ghia Contribution:  Driveable model of Lynx SS based on VW Scirocco components.
                    Included rumbleseat.
```

### What were they thinking...
When I'm writing or researching, I try to imagine what readers will think. Will they be surprised; will they smile; or, for example, will they wonder what on earth was Ghia's Erika Rumbleseat on Page 144? So here it is: the world's only three-seater Escort with a pop-up seat in the rear. OK, it's probably a bit of a letdown, but now you know. The two-seater Erika half-fascinates, half appalls me. Here are all the images. Notice how the file references that it was built over VW Scirocco mechanicals — yet another fully-drivable Ghia we never saw.

# THE TWO FACES OF ERIKA

*Courtesy Steve Aylen*

### Two men walked into a pub and....
I was told a story by an Australian editor of a British car magazine, whose name I shall protect. Back in 1979, he had been given a set of images of the upcoming Erika Escort in a mysterious meeting in a London pub. The instruction was to "Publish drawings of these pictures – the Americans are trying to change our car!" Here's what was going on behind the scenes... In late '77, the Erika Escort was well underway but the US version (top) needed different bumpers and lights for various legislative reasons. Both versions were being designed in Europe but US design boss Gene Bordinat was pushing for something glitzier. These pictures show the two cars looking similar, but within a year each would spiral off in different directions. Naturally someone – let's call him Henry – wanted the cars to look the same and by that he meant the same as the US Erika – hence the exchange in a beer-stained bar. The European Erika still has some way to go in this picture; notice the more formal-looking front and the different rear. In production, Erika was praised for its bustle back and the third pane of side glass, both missing here.

# THE FIRST SIERRAS VENTURE OUT

The Sierra, codenamed Project Toni, was a little late getting started because its predecessor Project Linda – the intended Taunus/Cortina replacement – was cancelled after a year's-worth of work. A new, more sophisticated RWD car for the '80s was about to dawn. Now that the first hand-built prototypes were up and running, the engineers and designers needed management direction for where to take it in the coming decade. The XR4i and Cosworth we all know about, but they created many more unseen derivatives, revealed in the pages ahead. It wasn't just the Sierra but the whole Ford range that was in for a sporting spruce-up, including an RS-style send-off for the Cortina that was far more interesting than the pipe-and-slippers Crusader model beloved of *Daily Express* readers.

### And they're off…
Designer Adrian Morris and I really wanted to have these images in *Secret Fords* but ran out of space, so here they are. This sequence shows the first Toni Sierra slithering down a wet track at Lommel in 1980. It's tempting to imagine the test driver throwing the car sideways moments later, but it's more likely that he took it easy. Engineers, rather than test drivers, usually drive test cars at first, feeling their way with such early cars constructed out of hundreds of handmade parts.

RS ICONS EDITION **041**

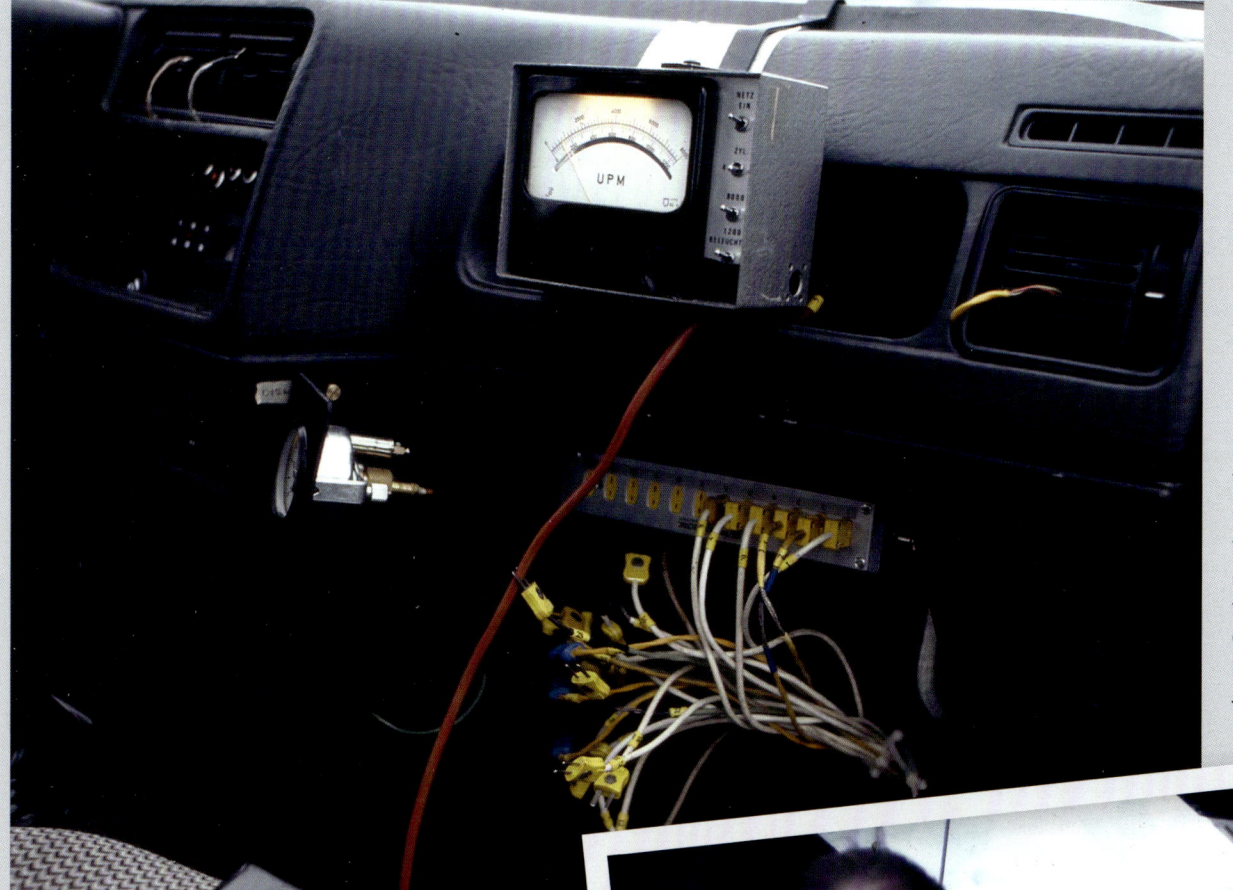

**Not what's needed**
This man has the world's largest rev counter. He's looking under the bonnet and trying to figure out how to tell his bosses that the 2.3litre version of the Granada engine just won't cut it. Notice the lack of chassis plate – that's an early bodyshell.

**Cutting a dash**
Today's test cars are very sophisticated – and yet simple to use. Many of the sensors that were used on a development vehicle like this XR4i are now standard. Braking force, air temperature, humidity, lateral G – chances are your car measures them while simultaneously linked to a cellular connection you don't even know about. Back in 1981, things were a little different. This first XR4i has a large oil pressure gauge bolted to the side of the dash and is festooned with sensors. Today, testers just plug their measuring equipment into the wiring harness.

# BOB'S FAVOURITE CHILD

Bob Lutz is one of the heroes of the car industry from his time at BMW, Ford, Chrysler and GM. Without him there would be no BMW kidney grilles, Dodge Viper or 2000s Pontiac GTO – or Sierra. I spoke to him a few years ago about Sierra. "Honestly, it's my favourite programme," he said. "Henry Ford II hated that car and I had to endlessly show him photos of sleek Citroëns, Porsches and Audis. The thing is that it was just so ahead of its time – but God, did Ford do well out of it, because it lasted 10 years without looking dated."

**And Henry said...**
Gerhard Hartwig, head of Vehicle Engineering, stands between two giants, Henry Ford II and Bob Lutz. Henry looks at one of the earliest Tonis and grunts "Will this thing sell?" Gerhard keeps his eyes down while Bob frantically prepares a reply. Or, just insert your own caption.

RS ICONS EDITION **043**

# IF SIERRA GAVE BIRTH TO A NEW CAPRI

Capri, Sierra and RS cars are some of my favourite fast Fords, so I couldn't believe my luck when I found this car in Ghia's archives. I showed it to Patrick le Quément, the man who oversaw the Sierra through to production. "Nope, never seen that one, and you know – it's really good!" he said. "It's typical, though, of what Ghia would do: squirrel away in secret and coming up with things like this." It's sure to offend those Capri enthusiasts who have a very firm view of what a Capri looks like but I give Ghia 9/10 for trying – which is why it's on the cover of *Secret Fords Volume One*.

**Could've, should've?**
Ghia's Sierra-derived Capri almost deserved a chance. These are all the photos, along with those in *Secret Fords*, that exist of the car. If one outlined the concept of making a Capri using the Sierra's design language to early '80s enthusiasts, they might have snorted in disgust. But would they have done so if they had seen this?

# THE PAPER THAT RESHAPED THE RS WORLD

Soon after the Fiesta RS faded away in late '79, Ford of Europe boss Bob Lutz dreamt up the idea for a Skunk Works to create fast-to-market special vehicles. The Motorsport group was able to create 100 or 200-off specials but Ford is in the thousands-per-day business. What he needed was a Special Vehicle Engineering team that was – unlike Motorsport – attached to the mainstream Vehicle Engineering group. The new team would be able to access the mainstream resources, supplier specifications and contacts, plus its test and development facilities. Most crucially of all, it would be within a few minutes' walk or drive from Design and Product Planning at the Dunton R&D centre.

The newly formed group's first special vehicle was developed under the project name Capri 2.8 FI Supersport. The Supersport tag had been applied to a limited run of Fiestas festooned in RS Series X Parts so it was initially used in lieu of a production name for what became the Capri 2.8 Injection. The fuel injected Capri was initially conceived using the same sprinkling of RS goodies as the Fiesta: Recaro seats, four-spoke RS wheels and Series X spoiler. Initial thinking was that it might be LHD only for the German market, which had a far less romantic attitude to RS. Things changed in summer 1980 when this paper was written by one of the Marketing team – the Capri was to be developed in RHD, with a provisional plan to sell it through British RS dealers.

It's a fascinating insight into future plans for Ford's sporting and RS vehicles and in the following pages we will look in detail at a few of these might-have-beens.

1. A relatively simple add-on to the existing Capri 2.8i programme – adding RHD was a no-brainer. In the years ahead the Brits loved the Capri more than any other market.

2. As with the Capri Injection, there was a consideration to sell the second version of the Fiesta Supersport through RS dealers – but the XR2 name was mooted early on. It made sense to permit Ford dealers to sell it alongside the Escort XR3.

3. Ford of Britain was so large that it could easily demand special vehicles for the British market. Turn the page to see what this RS-leaning Cortina might have be.

4. Ford of Germany – like its British sister – would order up a succession of Special Value Programs (SVPs). This first one for the Fiesta never happened. It was to be a tie-in with a designer 'name' like Gucci, or another fashion brand.

5. Capri 'dress up' – a Ford term for adding exterior styling features. See Page 51.

6. Granada think tank – presumably an open question of what could be added to the upcoming Scorpio, or existing Granada in its remaining years.

7. 4-wheel Drive – the Audi Quattro AWD had been revealed a few months earlier and the clear-thinking product planners knew it would be the future. The earlier AWD rallycross Capri was the right idea, just the wrong car at the wrong time.

8. Cabriolet/Targa – the Sierra was the next new car in the range, so naturally thoughts turned to an open-top version of this upcoming model. See pages 72 to 73.

9. Turbocharging – as quaint as it seems now, when nearly every piston-engined car uses the technology, forced induction was still a novel concept that carried prestige in the '80s. Even today, Americans say they plan to "turbocharge" something when they wish to imply that something will increase measurably.

# Selection of Next Special Vehicle Program

**POTENTIAL 1981 PROGRAMS**      Estimated Timing a/

1. RHD Version of Capri 2.8i — 6 months

2. Fiesta "Supersport" with worthwhile performance increment (1.1 or 1.3 with twin carbs or 1.6) — 9 months

3. Ford Britain Cortina "Super Ghia" — 9 months

4. Ford Germany Fiesta Designer Series — 9 months

5. Capri 2.8i Dress-up -- exterior moldings and spoilers and unique interior centre console — 9-12 months

**LONGER TERM PROGRAMS**

6. Granada "Think Tank"

7. 4-Wheel Drive

8. Cabriolet / Targa

9. Turbocharging

a/ Estimated timing from approval/start Engineering to Job One. Earliest start Engineering for next program is October 1980. SV Engineering resources do not permit concurrent development of two or more programs.

# CORTINA SUPER GHIA

Of course, there never was an RS Cortina. This is the closest we got. The collective 'we' were the few lucky South Africans able to buy a Cortina XR6 fitted with the Capri's 3.0litre V6. They liked it so much that a six-cylinder Sierra XR6 followed and then the mighty eight-cylinder XR8s seen on Pages 186 and 187 of *Secret Fords Volume One*. Unlike its African counterparts, Ford Motorsport in Europe never found a competitive use for the Cortina but was happy to sell go-faster goodies like spoilers, Recaro seats and RS wheels for it. The car pictured is the rarest version of the XR6, the XR6 Interceptor which gorged on the RS Parts brochure.

Ford of Britain had a different need back in summer '80. The chrome-laden Cortina 2.3 Ghia with standard-fit automatic gearbox was a plush thing that sold to older men who didn't want a higher-spec Granada. That wasn't good enough for someone in Ford of Britain's product planning team who set about creating the Cortina Super Ghia. The 3.0litre V6 was no longer emissions compliant and fitting the newer 2.8i engine would have cannibalised Granada sales at a time when both cars were getting old.

So, to tackle Alfa Romeo and BMW with a compact premium sports saloon, the planners drew up a list of every conceivable interior and exterior bauble, sweeping up every RS part and upmarket trinket along the way. The result would have looked the part: dechromed, with metallic black paint like a rapper's special from the decades to come. Read the spec in detail to see just how much effort went into creating this RS/Ghia mash-up that lacked for nothing — at least on paper.

*Courtesy Cars.co.za/SentiMETAL and Justin Pinto*

### Exterior changes over Cortina Ghia

- Metallic black paint
- Front spotlights
- Headlamp washers, and wipers from the Swedish Escort
- RS Series X front and rear spoilers
- 14-inch BBS wheels, or RS four-spoke with 195/60 Pirelli P6 tyres
- Unique red tape stripe
- Delete badges – final name TBD
- Roof-mounted aerial
- Black bumpers and window trims from Base Cortina
- Remote boot release

RS ICONS EDITION  047

### Interior changes over Cortina Ghia

- Granada Cool Black interior colour
- Granada Shark Grey trim and carpet colours
- RS2000 instrument pack
- Rear set headrests
- Rear seat belts
- Scheel RS seats with matching special velour fabric front and rear (unique)
- Cloth headlining and sun visors (unique)
- Centre console with velour lid and carpet sides (unique)
- Velour door tops (unique)
- Carpeted rear parcel shelf (unique)
- Door ajar working lights (unique)
- Electric rear view mirrors (unique)
- Cruise control (unique)
- Electric front windows (unique)
- Central locking (unique/Granada)
- Additional sound insulation (unique)
- Delayed action courtesy lights (unique)

RS ICONS EDITION  049

The interior was a product planner's dream team of features, ideas and components that would have moved the Super Cortina's interior as far from the wood-trimmed clubbiness of the Ghia as possible and deep into RS territory. It is natural to assume that the RS buyer was all about the driving experience, kissing corner apexes and roaring off down the straights. But no; Ford research showed that the interior ambiance of an RS had to be relatively plush, defined by unique fabrics, seats and instruments. Whoever conceived the Super Ghia knew what they were doing, working hard with Dunton's interior Colour & Trim design team to mix RS cues with premium features.

Special Vehicle Engineering needed direction for each of the potential projects and this one was the first to fall — the volume and profit potential of the Fiesta XR2 and RHD Capri Injection were just too great and left no room for others. This meticulously conceived Cortina Super Ghia would have taken Ford dealers into a new, more premium niche with Cortina, but it was a risk so close to the end of the car's life. Look at the long list of unique parts and see why SVE's efforts were better spent elsewhere than on this RS-inspired car that would have been hampered by humdrum standard engines.

Ford was looking forward to the upcoming Sierra. The first prototypes were about to hit the track and there was little point in reheating the ashes of an old car when its replacement was up and running. Alfa Romeo and BMW would have slept easily in their beds whether this Cortina had been launched or not. Better that it existed on paper, rather than lingering in a dealer's showroom? Probably.

*Courtesy Cars.co.za/SentiMETAL and Justin Pinto*

# PRODUCT PLANNING – A GAME PLAYED ON PAPER

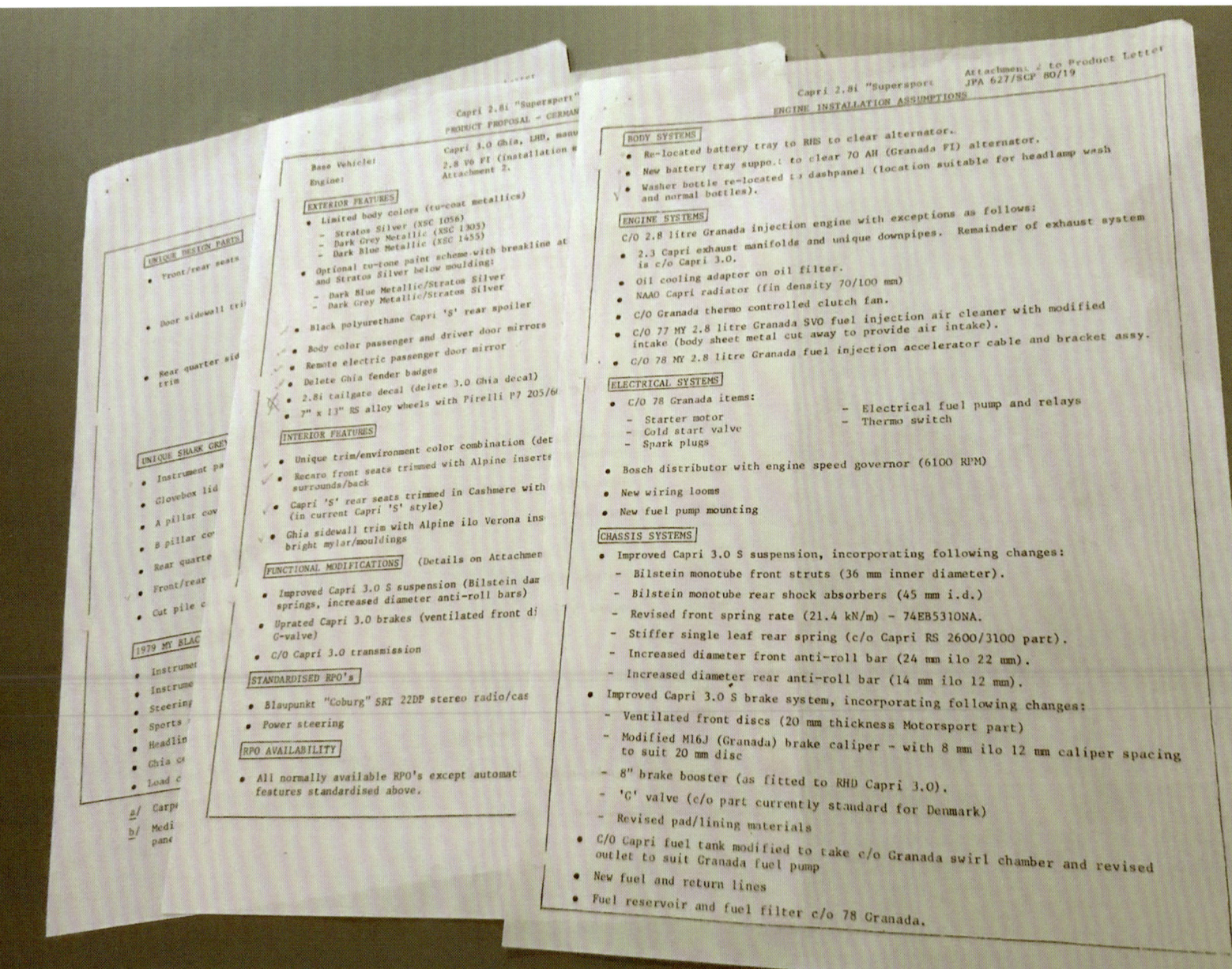

**Spot the difference**

The 2.8 Injection Capri was so close in spirit to an RS that there was some discussion about selling it through RS dealers. These are the three pages outlining the car when it was first conceived. Have a good look and spot the tiny differences to the car that was finally launched.

# THE CAPRI INJECTION YOU NEVER PROMISED YOURSELF

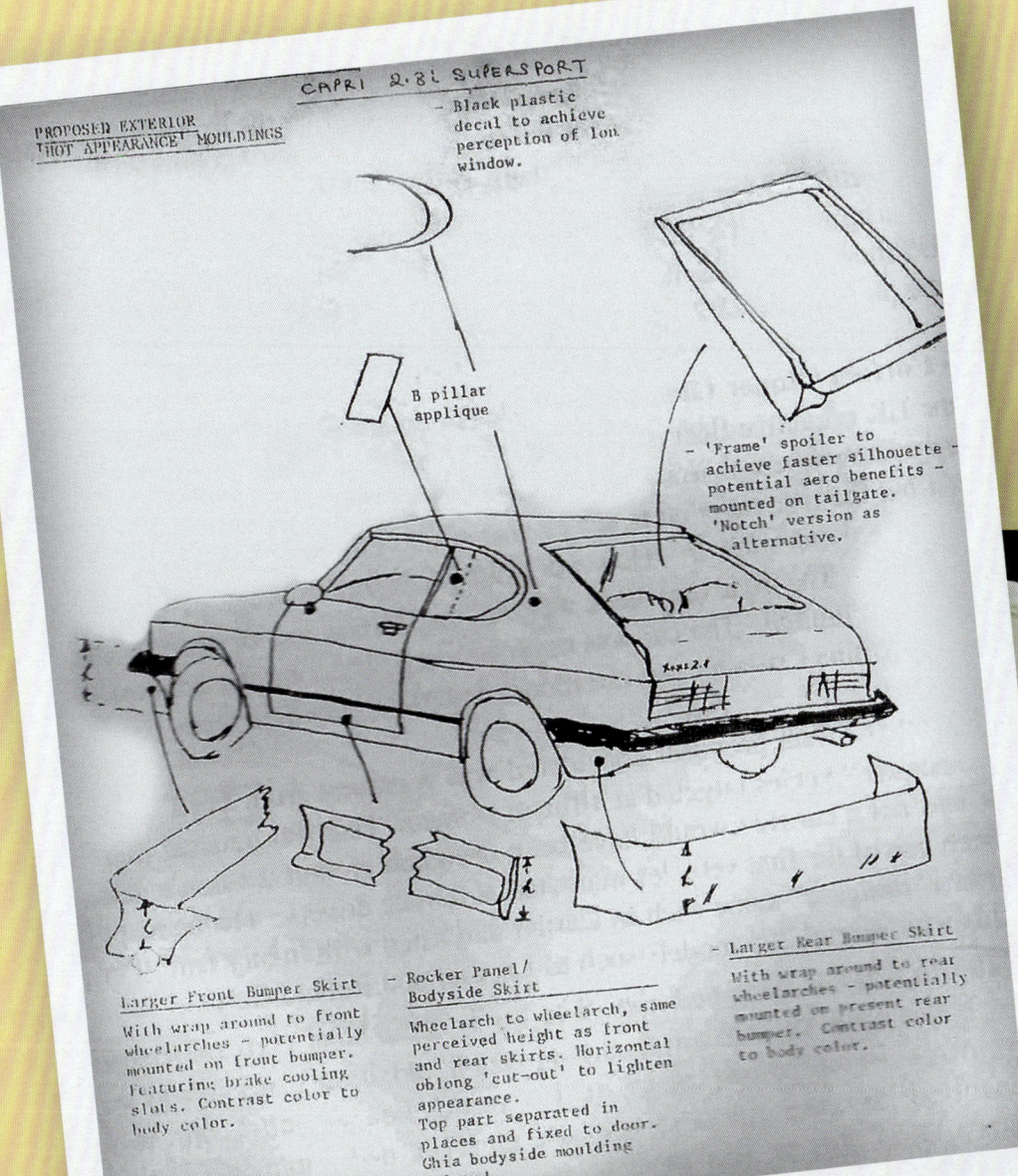

### The da Vinci road

After moving fast to engineer the Capri Injection, when the engineers began looking at follow-up programmes they considered a 'Capri Hot Appearance'. In plainer English that was little more than an aero kit and a centre console. Here's an SVE engineer's drawing, and a rendering of it from the rear by Karl-Heinz Nottrodt. Some engineers draw like Leonardo da Vinci, but not all of them.

*Courtesy Car Design Archives*

# SPEZIAL BUT NOT SPECIAL ENOUGH FOR THE RS BADGE

### Opening acts
These limited run cars – the Capri 3.0 Spezial and the RS2000 Spezial (right) – came about through a happy set of circumstances. The German Ford Motorsport team was literally at the end of Henry Ford Strasse from the factory and adjacent to the Pilot Plant. This fortunate proximity of the three entities meant that part-built cars could be whipped off the line and up the road in minutes to the specialist team capable of hand-building preproduction cars and special runs like these. Factories hate building what they call 'deviations' but 100-off runs were possible. The downside was a more costly build process and the risk of damage while moving part-built cars around.

**Right idea, wrong time?**
The Capri *turbo* looks as at home on one of the steep banks at the Nürburgring circuit as the Group 5 car that inspired it. It was conceptually good but arrived a year or two too late and had the misfortune to be launched within months of the Capri Injection. Motorsport's RS1600i suffered a similar fate, arriving close on the heels of the cheaper and better-handling fuel injected Escort XR3i.

# RS IN SPIRIT IF NOT IN NAME

The Escort Mexico and this car, the rare German-market '81 Capri *turbo* share the dubious distinction of lacking RS branding. So was the Capri *turbo* an RS in spirit, if not name? The short answer is: yes. It was developed by the same Motorsport group that developed the somewhat forgotten Escort RS1600i. Not only that, but the special wide bodies were also built by Zakspeed, Ford's works team that constructed the mighty Group 5 600bhp turbo Capris that inspired this road car. I've touched on it before but never had the chance to tell its story in detail, so let's take the opportunity to set the record straight and make a confession why I briefly had a personal interest in it.

In the late '70s, the German Motorsport group in Cologne had a different approach to its British counterparts. Rather than sell kits of RS Parts for go-faster buyers to modify their cars piecemeal, it built various 100- and 200-off runs of 'Spezial' Escorts and Capris. Called out in Motorsport's distinctive tricolour blue flash, they looked the part and created a modest profit while adding a halo to these ageing cars. The trouble was that hand-building special machines this way is expensive. It gets worse the longer they sit in stock tying up capital, yet they are worth less once buyers start demanding a discount. Ford is in the business of making money not just cars and as appealing as these vehicles were – with their fancy interiors, bulging arches and mildly tuned engines – their appeal was limited when they cost Porsche or BMW money.

In 1980 the Motorsport team started to think laterally. It needed more powerful engines and turbocharging was all the rage. Michael May was a Swiss engineer of some renown who had worked with Porsche and Ferrari before finding a ready market turbocharging the Cologne 2.3litre V6 carburetted Capri sold in Germany but not the UK. The Motorsport team initially thought of making a Granada Spezial but it was obvious that any higher performance engine using May's turbo kit needed to go into the Capri. It was a no-brainer; the Zakspeed Group 5 turbocharged 600bhp Capri racer was highly successful and the existing 3.0litre Capri Spezial looked for all the world like an RS car inside and out – it just needed more power.

Initial tests with a Capri centred around the carb-fed 2.3litre engine because the larger 2.8litre unit had ceased being installed in the US-market Capri a few years earlier. Things didn't go quite to plan; aftermarket kits have their limitations when faced with Ford's rigorous test schedules for emissions and durability. Inevitably there were engine failures due to overheating and the 2.3 turbo Capri was heading towards limited production. Then, in January '81, the pfennig dropped now that the specification for SVE's British designed Capri Injection was available. It incorporated useful upgrades to the cooling system, but the bigger fuel injected engine generated almost the same power as the blown 2.3 V6. Motorsport's Capri might look the part, but those bulging arches slowed it down and it was obvious that a turbo Capri costing 50 per cent more than a 2.8 Injection would be unsaleable.

The solution was obvious: upsize to the Granada's 2.8 carburetted engine and hope that buyers would be sufficiently wowed by the car's looks inside and out, the stiffly-sprung driving experience stemming from the RS3100-derived suspension and the sheer drama of the unique RS plenum chamber under the bonnet. Production started in August '81, with Zakspeed contracted initially to construct 50 wide-arched bodies from a planned run of 200 units in Cardinal Red, Diamond White or Strato Silver. The interior mirrored the contemporary Escort RS1600i by having a simple dark grey velour and RS steering wheel. The Capri *turbo* was only available in the German market and Switzerland, which carried over German homologation. An arcane rule which demanded that snow chains could be fitted meant – in theory – that steel 6.5-inch wheels were standard but in reality every car was fitted with the wider 7.5-inch items always intended to fill out the swollen arches.

Somewhat predictably the Capri *turbo*, launched within months of the Capri 2.8 Injection, struggled against its far cheaper, technically almost as interesting, and equally plushly-appointed sister. It is believed that just over 150 copies were sold, making it one of the rarest RS cars of all. Did it deserve the RS badge? Yes, certainly; it was simply a well-intentioned if somewhat misguided decision not to apply the two letters. Karl Ludvigsen, a PR man who briefly oversaw Motorsport, wanted the RS badge applied to cars with a pure competition focus. But have a good look around one of these cars and one sees it encrusted with entwined RS logos spoilers, wheels, seats, engine and many of the almost 200-odd unique parts fitted to this almost-mythical RS.

### Simple idea, complex in practice

A large amount of the Zakspeed racing team's labour – and overall cost – went into adding the flared arches to the Capri *turbo*. The part-built bodyshell was then sent back on the line for final assembly, with assistance from the Pilot Plant up the road. It was a dreadfully cumbersome – and so extremely expensive – way to make 200 planned-for cars.

### How many parts to make an RS?

It's natural to assume that the Capri *turbo* was simple to make because it used an adaptation of the Michael May turbo kit. Not really: each component had to be tested, modified if required and then a part number released into Ford's system. Then, spare parts had to be stocked and distributed through dealers as needed. Sounds easy in isolation but the engine, exhaust and fuel system featured no less than 49 unique parts *plus* another 26 components for the turbo installation. But that was just the engine componentry; in total there were 146 unique parts released by the Motorsport group to construct each car – well, 149 since it had four RS wheels.

*Courtesy Automobile.com*

### Telltail Whaletale

The gigantic front and rear spoilers were obviously inspired – like so much of the car – by Zakspeed's Group 5 racing Capri. The rear spoiler could be purchased separately for fitting to any Capri in the years that followed the Capri *turbo* ceasing to be made. Each rear spoiler came in a bag that contained a letter stating a strong warning (in German only) that it was essential to fit in conjunction with a matching front spoiler. The spoiler may have added extra downforce, but it had an unfortunate side effect; the gas struts supporting the tailgate were completely unable to cope with its extra weight.

### Sticker shock

BMW started it all. The old 2002 *turbo* used an italicised font to stress the urgency of forced induction powering its hot rod. Ford used the same style of italicised *turbo* script on the inlet manifold of the RS1700T's *turbo* engine. One can't but help wonder if adding the magic two letters to make this Capri the RS *turbo* might have resulted in sales reaching the 200 predicted, rather than just over 150.

### Oval pipes

Flattened oval twin exhausts had been a feature of the older Capri RS2600 and RS3100. They looked good and added a nice dash of practicality by providing a few extra millimetres of ground clearance. It's a wonder they haven't been picked up as a design theme by others. That is until one realises fluted pipe ends change the flow of the escaping gases and theoretically could add back pressure – that is unless they are being blown down the pipes by a turbo.

*Courtesy Auctomobile.com*

### Inside the unicorn

Keen RS-spotters will recognise the Scheel seats, and RS steering wheel, that were also fitted to the Escort RS1600i and the RS Spezial Escort and Capri seen a few pages earlier. It was an attractive-looking trim pack based on the Injection's with RS-branded Scheel seats and steering wheel. But the velour fabric on the seats used a foam-backing that would degrade over time, leaving them looking more worn and baggier than they were.

### Four-spoked perfection

There is a little tiny clue on these wheels. Peer closely and they bear the part number H75EB-1007-AA. As meaningless as that sounds, it tells all. The H denotes that they are a RS part and released in '75 for Capri (EB). Yes, these were the wheels intended for the cancelled RS2800. In theory, these alloys were optional and 5.5-inch steel items were standard to allow snow chain fitment, but of course every buyer wanted these wider 7.5-inch masterpieces.

The idea of a turbocharged 2.8 Capri was too good to ignore. If you could sort out the brakes, then a 200-plus bhp Capri was as much fun as a Lotus Esprit. And I should know, for I've run both. Ford sanctioned the fully type-approved RHD-only Tickford Capri a year-or-so after the LHD Capri *turbo*, eventually leading the Aston spin-off to become Ford Motorsport's partner on many projects. The second 'official' turbo Capri suffered from a high price point though and sold even *fewer* cars – just 100 – than the Capri *turbo*. In the third, and final, roll of the turbo Capri dice, Ford of Britain Marketing approved dealer fitment of the popular Turbo Technics kit. Third time lucky: low cost, low-lag, simple, effective, and justifiably popular – it was probably the best of the three. However, the Capri *turbo* always intrigued me. Quite by chance, I saw this white car pictured listed for sale in Switzerland in March 2020. This unicorn had covered something like a documented 32,000km in 39 years and nobody seemed to know about it; surely this car was perfect for me? But notice the date: it was the middle of COVID, Brexit and I was 3400 miles away from Switzerland unable to see it, transport it or store it. That turbo Capri is my RS that got away. Maybe one day I'll get to drive one?

# UNICORNS UNCOVERED

When I started talking to John Wheeler, the engineer behind the RS1700T, he was optimistic that he could find some unseen photos of the RS1700T in his loft. When he did find these images, I was overwhelmed and instantly enlarged the size of the book. Just look at this picture of John and designer Thomas Plath: there's a flight simulator cockpit looking on, a product of Specialised Mouldings where the car was created in secret. Thomas, in turn, was as excited as any 20-something when he was telling me about the car he crafted 40 years ago. He found the supplier a bit rough and ready, with clay modellers who weren't at the level of Ford's. It didn't stop him creating a masterpiece though. There were so many images left over that they spawned the idea of this scrapbook. I couldn't leave pictures like this to sit on my Mac forever, or have two hours of Facebook-fame. These pictures, like the car, deserve more than that.

*Courtesy John Wheeler*

RS ICONS EDITION **059**

### Essex wide boy
Somebody thought that the RS1700T needed wide arches and tried them for size on the clay model, P3. They sort of work, too. The photo on Page 220 of Secret Fords sits on the side window here, so we know P6 had been made at this point. Mercifully, this went no further and Thomas Plath's masterpiece was left untouched.

### The Prince and the Fin
In *Secret Fords Volume One*, two photos on Page 215 show Prince Michael of Kent walking up to the second mule, P5. They don't reveal who the driver was, but this shot does. The prince is beside Pentti Airikkala as the Fin hurls the RS1700T sideways.

## A MULE OUT TO PLAY

The first two drivable RS1700T mules, designated P4 and P6 (registered WVW 100W and WVW 101W) were proof-of-concept vehicles. P4 was powered by a naturally aspirated Hart Formula 2 engine while P6 had a BDA motor under the bonnet. P4 helped establish the overall viability of an Escort converted to RWD while P6 provided a benchmark for what the rally car could do – the raison d'être of the RS1700T.

*Courtesy John Wheeler*

### Hiding in plain sight
This shot was taken in Portugal in March '82 when Ford Motorsport decamped in secret to run prototypes P7 and P10 in a confidential test. Notice that the Transit support vans carry no Ford livery. To the right of the shot lurks WTW 569S. Although it too has no sponsor decals, it was actually Hannu Mikkola's 1979 RAC Rally winner, the last works RS1800.

## Stick in the mud

This was the RS1700Ts first venture outside of the confines of Boreham's locked gates. Usually, Ford Motorsport's support vehicles would be liveried in decals, but not this time. Mule P6, the second car to run was dispatched to the Welsh forests surrounded by plain clothed Transits, a Granada estate and WTW 569S, a full works spec Group 4 Escort. The blue tarpaulin hid the car from passing helicopters but the attendance of Bilstein's support vehicles and five Essex-registered plain white Fords might have given the game away.

**062** Secret Fords

### Days of Pentti
This was P10, the car used to set up engine calibration for the fuel-injected, turbocharged BDA engine. Staff from clutch and brake manufacturer AP Racing were in attendance to work with Boreham's John Griffiths to sort out the full-blown 400bhp rally engine with Dr Udo Zucker of Bosch. Works driver Pentti Airikkala then proceeds apace with no bonnet – a simple way of adding cooling and getting quick access to the engine.

### Five-spokes last stand
These attractive five-spoke wheels were fitted to the first RS1700Ts. However, designer Thomas Plath created an attractive seven-spoke design that was first seen on the FWD Escort RS1600i. Subsequent RS1700T prototypes adopted an eight-spoke version of the new RS wheel.

### Master at work
Few drove the RS1700T. Even fewer had the god-like talents of Pentti Airikkala. Thankfully, a photographer was there that day, when he played until sunset amongst the gravel pits at Boreham.

RS ICONS EDITION **063**

Courtesy John Wheeler

**Road or race?**
P10 looks like a shiny new road car, well aside from having no bonnet. But it was built as a rally test car. This was the last of the Phase 1 cars using a standard Escort wheelbase, later RS1700Ts moved the front axle forwards by 45mm.

### Death row

Perhaps the saddest shot in *Secret Fords Volume One* is the one on Page 230 showing the RS1700Ts lined up on death row, with the final car, P17, nearest the camera. Here they are (right) from the other end with the carcasses of the slain P7 and P9 in the foreground while the main shot shows the survivors nervously awaiting their fate.

*Courtesy Paul Moulson*

### XR3 no more

This is the interior of P17, the last car to be made. It's a workmanlike place, with mismatched trim and an exposed gear linkage — keep fingers clear please. The transmission tunnel intrusion into what was intended as a space-efficient FWD car is clear in this shot. Most prototypes tend to be made in LHD and the RS1700Ts were no exception, although three of the road cars (P8, P9, P14) were built with RHD. Other RS1700Ts were converted from LHD during their time in South Africa after the project was cancelled.

### Forklifted off to South Africa

Before I got into cars I was fascinated by aircraft and, yes, you've guessed it, cancelled and secret planes. One of the photos I vividly remember was the row of abandoned TRS2s from 1965 — a cancelled bomber that overran on cost and underdelivered on performance. The incomplete airframes were taken out to the sands off Shoeburyness in Essex and used as target practice. Thankfully P12 didn't suffer from the same fate, despite the indignity of being forklifted into the back of a South African truck. It still survives to this day.

RS ICONS EDITION **065**

# RS1700T: THE QUIET SURVIVOR

When I wrote *Secret Fords Volume One*, RS1700T expert Paul Moulson and I spent many hours trying to figure out how many P-numbered cars there were. It wasn't easy! We concluded (see page 231) that there were 11 cars plus two mules. But there is a nuance here that makes us believe that total might be slightly lower. Look at the chart below and it's evident that some P-numbered RS1700Ts used the same registration number at different times; notably P9 – amongst others – appears out of sequence from their date of registration. It's not wholly unusual because, in a rally team, cars are often crashed and reshelled – sometimes with a new identifier, sometimes not.

What we do know is that there were 8 cars and quite possibly 11 – plus P4 and P6, the two mules. To add a little fun, and confusion on top, there were another three service shells that also made the trip to South Africa to join the four-or-so complete cars sent there. It is remarkable how many RS1700Ts survived their South African adventure and returned to the UK. Of the 8-11 cars made, an astonishing six cars/shells are accounted for. The tally increased after another surfaced in late 2021. Most prototypes are crushed but not the handful of RS1700Ts – although they had a troubled birth, around half survived. Not bad for a cancelled car.

|  | Usage | Original UK registration number | Afterlife | Colour |
|---|---|---|---|---|
| **P1** | RWD Fiesta BDA | PNO 613R | Registration later used on FWD Roger Clark rally Fiesta | |
| **P2** | Engine installation buck | | | |
| **P3** | Styling buck | | | White/clay |
| **P4** | Mule | W100 WVW | | |
| **P5** | Show car model | Unregistered | Supplied in green | White |
| **P6** | Rally car mule | W101 WVW | | White |
| **P7** | Rally car | W101 WVW | Registration from P6 and crashed by Vatanen | White |
| **P8** | Road car | DVW 420X | Written-off | Red |
| **P9** | Road car | FPU 737Y | | White |
| **P10** | Rally car | W100 WVW | Registration from P4, now UK-owned | White |
| **P11** | Unknown | DVW 421X? | | |
| **P12** | Road car | FPU 738Y | Believed running gear fitted to one of three spare shells | White |
| **P13** | Road car | FPU 739Y | | White |
| **P14** | Unknown | | | |
| **P15** | Road car - engine calibration | FPU 740Y | Owned by Malcolm Wilson | Blue |
| **P16** | Rally car | GJN 736Y | | White |
| **P17** | Rally car | Unregistered | Last reported in US | White |

P16 and P17 were built from five preproduction-level shells. P18, P19 and P20 would have probably have been constructed from the next three shells in series. Two of the remaining three spare shells have been used to make running cars.

Errata. *Secret Fords Volume One* Page 233 swaps P5 with P6 and it is now thought that the car marked there as P10 is more likely to be P16.

RS ICONS EDITION **067**

### The definitive RS1700T
This is P15, a completely standard road-spec RS1700T that was used by SVE and represents the RS1700T in as definitive form as could be. Like the other surviving cars, it went to South Africa with the intention of being rallied. But nobody seemed to have the heart to rip out the road car interior and chop it about. It is owned by Malcolm Wilson, former works driver and now the owner of M-Sport, which delivers Ford's rallying effort today.

# THE THREE-DOOR SIERRA: FORD'S HERO WITH HUMBLE ROOTS

The doomed RS1700T couldn't escape twin curses: it was conceived just as the Audi Quattro started winning rallies; and its developers faced the Herculean task of converting a FWD family hatchback into a RWD Group B supercar. Ford Motorsport would soon be under new executive leadership – this time it was blessed with better fortune: in late '82, the new RWD Sierra was up and running.

So the ingredients were there but the best way of serving the next RS dish would take time to identify and then to cook.

Back in the '70s Ford and many other manufacturers offered two-door versions of their entire ranges from top to bottom, Granada down to Fiesta. Although two-door versions of the Taunus/Cortina and Granada added manufacturing complexity,

**Genesis of Sierra**
This full-sized model dates to 1978. Although the pillar angles are wrong, it still looks like the production car that would follow in five year's time. Notice the five-door configuration on the far side.

**Green machine gets the nod**
The Sierra was signed off using this full-sized fibreglass model in October '79, again with a three- and five-door configuration on either side. The spec shows a three-door Ghia that would never make production. Instead, the concept of the three-door Sierra was split into two. This shell was now reserved exclusively for the XR4i.

they also attracted different customers and thus incremental sales — it was a neat trick. The larger two-door Taunus/Cortinas and Granadas didn't appeal to British buyers but German Ford buyers had a longstanding desire for them. At the budget end of both model's ranges, buyers enjoyed slightly cheaper vehicles that locked children safely in the back, unable to escape their parents' ABBA tapes. At the more premium end, far more profitable coupes could be made by using the same two doors and chopped-down rears. A pair of additional spin-off derivatives for less than the price of a whole separate new one — genius.

**Looking down on something new**
The three-door Sierra looks best from this angle (see also page 87). It is a view that maximises the area where the shell differs the most from the regular five-door.

**The new face of fast Fords**
This was the XR4i as Thomas Plath conceived it, complete with wide wheels that filled out the arches and an F1-style rear spoiler with end plates. An earlier version of this rendering shows it with quad lights intended for the North American derivative.

So when the hatchback-only Sierra programme, codenamed Project Toni, kicked off in 1978 there was a need to create a three-door alongside the mainstream five-door and estate. German designer Gert Hohenester was always known for his flurries of radical ideas and, with his vision for Project Toni, he reached a peak. His earliest sketches included a three-door featuring three side windows, known as a six-lite style in Ford's American-English dialect. It was certainly radical but it passed unchanged through the design process as a simple three-door and not as a sporty, coupe-like car. But in early '81 there was a change of heart. Ford of Europe boss Bob Lutz had a huge hit on his hands with the smaller Escort XR3 and started pushing for the six-lite car to be turned into a sporty XR4, one size up. Cunning as Bob was, he saw a huge opportunity to send the car stateside where it could sell on its German heritage and futuristic looks. In a clever bit of product planning and positioning, the XR4 could be sold as a new European competitor to the BMW 3 Series in North America

This left Ford of Europe in a quandary. The six-lite shell couldn't really be a sporty XR4 *and* a basic model at the same time. There was an obvious solution: the extra pillar limited rear seat passenger visibility, so removing it and replacing the two rear side windows with one large single pane was a relatively low-cost way

### Flare-arched RS
When the XR4i exterior design was finished in late '81, Ford's designers began freeing up their minds to envisage what might come next. This wonderful rendering by Wolfgang Gotschke has a wider body with flared arches and a whimsical RS badge. Within two years the team would be designing an RS Sierra for real.

of adding a fourth body to the forthcoming Sierra line-up – then still two years from launch. It would take time to make the giant body side dies to stamp out the four-lite shells, so it arrived almost a year after the rest of the Sierra range.

The original plan had been for the XR4 – renamed XR4i late in the day to sync with that of the new fuel-injected Escort XR3i – to use a 2.3i engine. But tests proved that, with 130bhp, it was incapable of making the car fast enough so the capacity was upped to 2.8litres. In mid '81, RS1700T designer Thomas Plath was tasked with creating a new character for the XR4i, distinct from the regular family man's five-door Sierra. Thomas did it, and then some, with a quad-lamp front that met North American regulations and an F1-style rear wing complete with endplates, and wide tyres nestling flush against the aerodynamic shrouding along the sides. There was so much freshness and hope in Thomas's design, even when it was watered down with narrow tyres to raise top speed by reducing drag, and ditching the quad lights initially inspired by the US version. The biggest change was the addition of the biplane rear spoiler – although it defined the car for most, it was donated by the Probe III show car designed alongside it that summer.

### The mercurial face of Sierra
The North American Sierra was conceived when a local law dictated standard-sized square headlights. The idea was that it allowed an unlucky motorist to pop into any parts store or garage to buy a replacement. Thankfully the law was changed before the Merkur XR4Ti was launched. This full-sized model incorporates a never-seen logo with an 'M' under an outline image of Cologne Cathedral. The flowing door mirror didn't make the cut either.

By mid '82, the XR4i was headed to production but the designers hadn't quite let go and gave the lemon one more squeeze to drip out a fifth body style, or arguably six if you counted the US-market version, which had so many unique parts that it had to be made by coachbuilder Karmann. Ford designer Wolfgang Gotschke sketched up some ideas for adding more spice, like a wide-bodied RS although that wasn't in the brief. No; the designers had something far more surreal in mind.

The Capri was ageing fast and although the 2.8 Injection model gave it new life, sales were inevitably going to fizzle to zero by '85. Someone had a bright idea: why not tackle the Capri market by expanding the XR4i into a range of versions? A low cost 2.0litre injection XR4i five-door and — most bizarrely of all — a two-door Targa. The targa/cabriolet idea, first mooted two years earlier in summer 1980, was now moving forward apace as a new project for SVE under Geoff Fox, who smiles at the recollection. "It was almost tongue-in-cheek in because I can't imagine there would have been a huge market for it," he says. That wasn't going to stop designer Tom Jara in February '82 when he began experimenting with a novel forward-leaning C-pillar that swept forwards to form a T-bar with a central roof spar. A Saab-like rear spoiler jutted out the back to offset the visual weight of the rear folding roof that replaced the hatchback. It was an extraordinary thing that shouldn't work in theory but, thanks to some

**Sunny side up**
Designer Tom Jara captured the spirit of the Sierra Targa in these picture-perfect renderings. Correct in almost every detail, except for the Saab-like rear spoiler that was absent on the final full-sized model. Look at the Mediterranean vibrancy of the colours and imagine this car wafting through the south of France or Italy. Even if one doesn't like the idea behind the car, it's impossible not to admire the quality of the artwork.

impressive renderings it – like the normal XR4i – had something intriguing about it.

A full-sized model was finished down to the tiniest detail by October '82 and a decision about pressing the button or not needed to be made. This was the same month that the Sierra was launched, and Ford soon found that the vehicle's design was polarising – better to wait and see if the three-door XR4i was well-received before decapitating it into a two-door Targa. Unfortunately, Ford rapidly discovered it had trusted the designers to push things too much. Journalists and customers alike thought the XR4i was too extreme in looks relative to its driving experience. The grey bodyside cladding and red stripes were seen as cheap looking. That was easily addressed. The bigger issue was that it lacked the dynamic thrills of the same-engined Capri Injection and had a long list of options that drove up the price. Ford had a dud on its hands and the car lasted less than two years in Europe, while the North American Merkur version plodded on for three years longer.

By spring '83, the Targa was dead; Ford had other priorities – it needed to work fast to reboot the Sierra. The XR4i had stumbled but it was evident that something more dramatic would be needed. Ghia in Italy created what it called a 'Sierra Luxury Convertible' that aped the Mercedes SL with a dash of Audi. Nice try, but something more heroic was needed as an emphatic statement that the Sierra could be a winner.

**Ready to roll down**
This silver model was finished in October '82, the very month that the Sierra was launched. The designers wisely painted the aero kit in body colour and finished the model off with a TARGA logo that replaced the SIERRA decal. Many of the images in *Secret Fords* are models, often so convincing that it is impossible to tell they are not the real thing. Well, not this one: peer inside – there is no interior!

# WHEN SIERRA MET MERCEDES

Bob Lutz came up with the idea of fighting BMW in the US by creating a new brand, Merkur, to sell the XR4 and Scorpio there. He envisaged the cars being sold not through Lincoln-Mercury or Ford dealers, but by independent outlets that specialised in imported cars. The reality was somewhat different; the Merkur franchise was awarded to big-selling Lincoln-Mercury dealers. Bob had responsibility for sales outside North America so could do nothing and Merkur limped along, avoided by the BMW-buyers the car was aimed at. What makes this Sierra-derived, SL-style, convertible so fascinating is that it wears a Lincoln rather than the Merkur badge it deserved. The two 1983 shots below were taken in Detroit, so it had been taken seriously enough to have been shipped over from Italy. But even though the German-made Merkur XR4s were just starting to be sent across, it seems that nobody had told Ghia. It was a tiny bit of evidence that not everyone was as supportive of the Merkur brand as Bob.

### Dallas Special

From the rear, there is an undeniable whiff of the Mercedes SL, immortalised by Bobby Ewing in the *Dallas* TV show. It's near-enough convincing and might have pulled it off. Ford was always keen to tackle GM products such as its new European-built Cadillac Allanté – this would have been its riposte. The American side of the house had another go at repurposing the Sierra chassis as few years later when it was briefly considered for the GN34 supercar featured in *Secret Fords Volume Two*.

RS ICONS EDITION  **075**

**Open-topped tailslider**
Although the Sierra Targa ground to a halt in late '82, Ford's North American arm was flush with cash and full of bravado and commissioned Ghia in Italy to create this oddball. The European side of the house was about to reinvigorate the Sierra's reputation via three sporty models, a 2.0iS for family motorists, the XR4x4 for everyday performance and the mighty RS Cosworth for RWD enthusiasts. But tail-out driving wasn't on the cards for many American convertible buyers in sunny southern states and – this was the '80s, remember – people in northern states were just waking up to the idea of AWD being almost essential in this size of car. When Cadillac launched its 4.1 litre Allanté it – rather perversely – opted for FWD.

# THE TAIL OF THE RS ICON

I told the story of the original whaletail Sierra Cosworth at length in my first book *The Cars You Always Promised Yourself*. I wished I'd had the space there to show this image and the two on the next spread. Here, we do have the room to do these never-seen images justice. I'll quicky reprise the story as we go, but just enjoy these photos along the way. They are all stunning.

RS ICONS EDITION 077

**Secret Fords**

The Sierra XR4i began its short life in spring 1983, just as thoughts started to be hatched about what to do with a next-generation evolution of the car. Stuart Turner had been reappointed Director of Motorsport recently by his friend, and now boss once more, the legendary Walter Hayes. As Stuart started his new role, he and Walter had had to endure watching the Capri being easily beaten to top honours at Silverstone by Rover, while the Escort RS1600i struggled to achieve a decent class win in its category. But Stuart had the answer. He cast around for support to make 5000 Group A Sierras after learning of a DOHC engine conversion for the Sierra's 2.0litre engine. Over a pub lunch with Ford and Cosworth bosses, Stuart explained how a turbocharged version could be a race winner. Now he just had to get it made and sold.

The idea gathered traction during the year and by autumn the product planning team issued a Product Letter to SVE instructing it to proceed with engineering the 200bhp Sierra. The car had one task: to win races. Ford had to design, engineer and sell 5000 copies, plus 500 evolution versions featuring even more specialised motorsport componentry. Time was tight: the facelifted and heavily revised Sierra would enter production in just over three years, meaning that the Group A Sierra with special aero mods was on a deadline the moment the project was given the green light in September '83.

The SVE team built two XR4i-based mules. The first – RST10, seen below – was used to determine the aero package while its sister, RST11, ran the first Cosworth YB engine installation. A key need was to develop the aero package by determining exactly what was needed and where. What combination and location of aero addenda created the right mix of downforce? The key was to make the aero package work when the car entered corners at an angle – a sudden change in air pressure would upset handing balance. It's natural to imagine that the only role of a spoiler is to push a car down at the rear, but the most effective ones reduce lift *and* help carry speed into a corner by adding stability. It's the reason why the Sierra – and the Escort Cosworth that followed – were never designed with three spoilers; the twin wing aero package was sufficient.

The first aero tests with RST10 were conducted at MIRA's Northamptonshire wind tunnel in early November '83 under the guidance of SVE's Gordon Prout. The practical SVE engineers promptly set about it with a pop-rivet gun and sheet aluminium as they looked for ways of adding downforce. The car was then shipped back to Germany with the 'best theoretical compromise' where racing driver Klaus Niedzwiedz tested its high-speed stability at the Nürburgring circuit. The aero package alone was found to be worth an extra 2mph, enough to give it a winning edge on the straights while adding grip and speed in the corners. It might have worked, but RST10 looked horrific: its pop-rivetted alloy spoiler kit needed to be cleaned up into something that 5000 enthusiasts might want to buy.

Now back home in Germany, the Cologne-registered XR4i was sent into the Merkenich wind tunnel, adjacent to the nearby design studio. It was refined into the form seen on these pages, retaining a certain brutish charm led more by engineering function than aesthetic form. It was time to let the Design team lend a hand. Nobody anticipated that its creation — swiftly worked up over three months in early '84 — would become one of the most recognisable designs of the next 40 years.

Dunton-based Uwe Bahnsen oversaw Ford's European design team while Patrick le Quément led the Cologne studio. Amongst the many stars in this crack team was Harm Lagaay, a former Porsche designer who would later go on to lead design at BMW Technik and then, after returning to Stuttgart, head Porsche design overall. Harm recalls: "I think they asked me to work on the car because they knew I loved motorsport and had done various 911 racers before. Plus, I was always hurtling around sideways in my 3.0litre Capri!" In February '84, the Dutchman and Japanese designer Ichiro Hatayama set about incorporating the key hard points of the aero kit in a style that matched the Sierra's complex design language.

**The first Sierra Cosworth**
RST10, the first Sierra Cosworth, was still powered by the XR4i's 2.8litre V6. Even with such limited power it was measurably faster on the track than the standard car. So the aero pack's key hard points had been established — the car had done its job and it was time for the design team to take over and create one of the most iconic cars Ford would ever make.

RS ICONS EDITION **081**

**Sportiness for all**
The Sierra 2.0iS, above, called simply 'injection' in some markets, was intended to offer Sierra buyers a sportier car at an affordable price by using a fuel-injected version of the wheezy 2.0itre SOHC engine. This design model retains XR4i badging and a modified biplane spoiler with a central support spar. Neither would reach production but we would see the idea for propping up the spoiler again.

**The profile of a classic begins to take shape**
The design brief called for the sportier XR4i's six-lite shell to be used. This is one of the first sketches, a full-sized tape drawing that concentrated on the rear spoiler style and flared wheelarches needed to cover 10-inch-wide racing rubber, with a rocker panel moulding linking the arches. It had a hard-edged, technical look but the Sierra used far more complex organic surfaces than this. Notice the use of Escort XR3i wheels – simple expediency in the absence of anything else.

082    Secret Fords

**Getting closer**
Ichiro Hatayama's sketch from March '84 looks far closer to the production car. The rear spoiler and side skirt style are in place. Now, it was time to transfer them on to a full-sized fibreglass model and start thinking about what form a revised front bumper should take.

## Body language

These images from mid-March '84 show the first pass at a full-sized model. It was created using one of the fibreglass XR4i models after the bodyside mouldings had been removed. One side featured seven-spoke RS wheels and the other full-blown BBS-style racer-width rims. The front bumper had been revised in line with Hatayama's sketch but it lacked the swagger and aggression expected of an RS car. Revising the bumper shapes demanded Lagaay's skill and knowledge of the Sierra's body language. He had been involved with the car from its earliest days and knew how section changes and subtle forms could dramatically influence it.

## Muscling-up to beat the best

Two weeks later and the car is transformed. The front bumper has been reprofiled with a square-jawed air intake and two different types of muscular brake air ducts on the left and right. The bonnet vents have evolved from being simple slots to rectangular items that echo the more muscular rectangular forms of the revised bumper. This is the Sierra RS Cosworth being born.

**The way it was meant to be**
This dramatic overhead shot was taken in the Merkenich design showroom, just two minutes' walk from where it was modelled earlier in the day. The angle hides the losing left side air intake and shows every feature of the revised aero kit to good effect. Design handed it over in this form to SVE for production in April '84. Just a few weeks later, the engineers were advised that the six-lite XR4i was to cease production. Therefore, the Sierra RS needed to adopt the plainer-looking four-lite shell from the Base and L models rather than the sportier six-lite body seen here. You be the judge: with 40 years hindsight, which of the window shapes works best? The smooth grille-less nose from the XR4i/Ghia was still retained at this stage and even in the first press shots Ford released: they used a converted Sierra 1.6L and also featured this front — that was until the engineers punched an extra cooling hole was into it.

RS ICONS EDITION **085**

**086** Secret Fords

### Plastic but still fantastic
This car, like the fibreglass Sierra Targa seen earlier, looks ready to roll but it too lacked an interior and the vented disc brakes peeping through the wheels were cardboard. The full-width race wheels were essential to help determine the stance of the racing version and provided inspiration for the road car's rims that would be designed some months later. Design was under pressure at the time after the Sierra's wobbly start but there was no doubting the strength of the talent involved. Harm Lagaay looks back affectionately at his creation, part of a portfolio that later included the BMW Z1, Porsche Boxster, several generations of 911 and the Carrera GT supercar. He says: "I really think I applied all my earlier Porsche thinking to the Cosworth – it could have been more over the top, but it has a nice sense of 911 restraint and style." There's ample design refinement to back Harm's assertion: look at the muscular arms that extend rewards to hold the tea tray spoiler and the sophistication of the colour eventually known as Moonstone Blue.

RS ICONS EDITION  **087**

### First of its kind to hit the road

This is RST12, the third prototype and the first to use the four-lite shell, with its two side windows, that featured both the new aero kit and the Cosworth engine. It was built in September/October '84, using handmade plastic and fibreglass panels. Just a year after the project had got the greenlight, the definitive Sierra RS Cosworth was up and running. Seven prototypes and two full-sized models later, the first preproduction Sierra RS Cosworths were headed down the line. After a few last-minute tweaks that delayed full-scale production until June '86, there was a frantic rush to make 5542 units before December that year because that's when production of the original Sierra stopped and the facelifted version took over.
Each Sierra RS Cosworth was painted Black or Diamond White while Moonstone Blue, the colour beloved of Design, was the rarest of all. Well not quite: one solitary Rosso Red example was sent down the line at the request of the Duke of Bedford, which is why it deserves its place on this book's cover.

### Race engines in road cars are not cheap

The numbers and figures YBB 025 hastily scrawled on a piece of tape say it all. This was the 25th engine to be made and the second to be installed in a running vehicle, after RST11 was sent off to Italy where the Magneti Marelli fuel injection system was designed. The engine, which cost half as much as a regular Sierra, went on to last well into the mid '90s, despite being based on the SOHC Pinto unit that dated back to the early '70s.

*Courtesy Don Liddard*

**Left abandoned for all to see**
I took this photo in summer 1985 at a Dunton open day when employees could bring their families to work. The prototypes, mainly uninteresting Fiesta 1.1s and Escort estates, were herded into a field at the back. I know because I helped drive some of them there. That's how I came to take this shot of RST12 sitting there abandoned and unloved. Ordinarily, one couldn't take a camera in to work but that day it was allowed, so I took the shot knowing it would be useful 40 years later.

# TWEEDLEDEE AND TWEEDLEDUM

These shots from the Nürburgring in early 1984 show several SVE employees ministering to the four Escort RS Turbos used for ride and handling development. The hot Escort was developed at speed alongside the Sierra RS Cosworth as part of Stuart Turner's plan to make three cars: an Escort for clubman's rallying, a Sierra for Group A racing and a specialised Group B rally car. The Escort RS Turbo was a far simpler project that called upon Motorsport and SVE's bank of knowledge to turbocharge and fuel inject the Escort. A simple car maybe, but one that sold well — 8000 copies during its 12-month life.

*Courtesy Peter Hitchins*

### Approach with care – and a long lens
Tweedledee and Tweedledum RS Turbo prototypes and the hapless SV15 seen on Page 257 of *Secret Fords Volume One*. If you ever wondered where a lot of the spy shots in magazines are taken, it's along the approach roads that lead into these Nürburgring garages. There's no point trying to shoot them on the track: the cars are too fast so spy photographers just wait by the roadside.

RS ICONS EDITION **091**

**Integral to the RS plot**
Four of the eight prototypes are in this shot. Note the Lancia Delta comparison car nearby. It's not an Integrale but an HF. The AWD Lancia didn't arrive until 1986.

# THE ITALIAN JOB FINISHED IN BRITAIN

The design story of the RS200 is told in detail in *Secret Fords Volume One*, so let's enjoy a quick reprise here and focus on these unseen photos. Creating the RS200 was an almost Herculean effort. Ford had to make 200 specialist Group B rally cars in a very short time. The task had eluded Boreham's John Wheeler first time around, with the RS1700T, but he'd been handed a gift this time. Rather than convert an existing car to meet Ford's top-flight rallying needs, his team would design and manufacture a purpose-built one that encapsulated a Ford look thanks to the adoption of the Sierra's windscreen and cut-down doors.

Ghia in Italy was selected for the job rather than the mainstream studio in Cologne. Several designers at the Turin studio submitted ideas but neither Mike Moreton in Ford Motorsport nor Filippo Sapino, Ghia's boss, liked what they saw. But one sketch, seen on page 264 of *Secret Fords Volume One* nailed it. Although Filippo hadn't drawn it, he ran with the shape and directed the look of the Ghia's full-sized model. Sapino had an impressive track record. His early work included the seminal Ferrari Modulo; and this one was undoubtedly a triumph, one that today's Ford design team still admires.

But it was no more than a model that needed building into a functional vehicle — *now* the hard work was about to begin. These never-seen photos take us from the first model through to the final 200th car.

**Perfect partnership of RS and Ghia**
The RS200 model under construction at Ghia's studio in Turin. Despite being owned by Ford for 30 years, the Italian design shop would only ever see two of its cars, the RS200 and the StreetKa convertible, enter production. Many of Ford's cars featured tiny Ghia crests on the side, but they were simply badges attempting to add a little designer cachet. The RS200 was the only production Ford to wear with complete justification the Ghia badge *and* RS logo.

**The quarter-million dollar bargain started here**
Ghia's RS200 model from late '83 looked like the real thing, but the smoked windows reveal that there was no engine or interior. Yet it was enough to gain the green light for the building of a single functional prototype, made for a mere $250,000, an absurdly low sum given the task. Project Manager Mike Moreton and Chief Engineer John Wheeler used a cunning combination of specialist fabricators and fibreglass moulding experts to build car 001 in just under six months.

094　Secret Fords

**Spoiling it by degrees**
This is Car 001 in the Merkenich wind tunnel in mid '84. Earlier tests had shown that the car's aero performance needed to add more stability at speed. Unlike the Sierra RS Cosworth, which had started by being developed in the wind tunnel eight months earlier, the Ghia designed RS200 was devoid of spoilers. Notice the giant circular plate with incremental degree markings: it was used to angle a vehicle into 130mph winds to see how it behaved away from the straight ahead. The tape along the A-pillar was used to simulate a tighter shutline than achieved on this first try-it-and-see car.

RS ICONS EDITION **095**

**Quick fixes add speed**
A makeshift front spoiler was hastily assembled from sheet aluminium and applied to the front of Car 001. The tests proved that, as pretty and fast-looking as the RS200 was, it needed revised body surfacing and an aero kit to help hold it down at speed and to cool the drivetrain.

Secret Fords

**Nothing to sniff at**
This is the revised version of Ghia's model, which was developed at Dunton under the direction of English designer John Hartnell and Scotsman Ian Callum. They created an interior for the car that was simple to make in LHD and RHD by using a mix of existing Ford parts and low-cost mouldings. After the wind tunnel tests, the exterior needed a makeover, too. Here, John stands in front of one the CE14 '91 Escort renderings on a board while taking to Director of Design Uwe Bahnsen (in the black suit) and sniffing-with-a-cold Andy Jacobson, who would soon take over from his boss. Callum and Hartnell completely made-over the exterior design, including incorporating Chief Engineer John Wheeler's updated requirements following rally and aero testing. After they were done, the car looked more workmanlike and ready for action than the slightly twee-looking iteration that had first arrived from Italy. Callum recalls: "I learned so much from working on that car with John, and when the need to help sort out the Escort Cosworth came along later, they gave it to me as a design task. I always loved these functional cars that were built for action."

## SNOW WHITE AND THE SIX PROTOTYPES

The RS200's Chief Engineer John Wheeler's recalls, "The Tickford project was basically taking the original motorsport-based design and completely designing, revising and improving it for "mass-production", manufacturing, legality, durability, road customer acceptability and manufacturing cost-effectiveness. It was a big project, involving every component of the car, and working with major manufacturing partners. I typically spent two or three days a week at Tickford working with the team there. Other major partners were FF Developments (complete transmission) Cosworth, JQF (engine), AP Racing (brakes and clutch), Arch Motors (chassis) and Reliant (composite body).

Meanwhile the rally car build and test program continued at Boreham with constant feedback to the Tickford and Design team for modifications to the body."

### RS with a dash of Aston

Tickford had proven its worth with the earlier Tickford Capri — a turnkey solution to getting a specialist vehicle tested and ready for the road. SVE was equally adept at developing such machines but better-suited to engineering thousands of specialist cars that could be made on the line. But just hundreds of unusual Fords, Jaguars or Rovers? Well, call Tickford. The inset photo is Car 001 working hard during durability testing in the snowy Welsh hills, and taking a breather in Tickford's workshop soon after. The Vauxhall Cavalier lurking in the background was another of Tickford's client projects. This adjacent shot shows Car 003 being put through its paces by Tickford's team at the Bruntingthorpe Proving Ground. The giant yellow plaster on its nose covers the Ford logo, indicating it was taken in late '84, before the world first saw this secret Ford at the Turin show that year.

*Courtesy Dave Boulton*

**098** Secret Fords

**Banking can be boring**
The image of a test driver is someone with Stig-like skills throwing a car around a track. The reality is very different. These pictures show Tickford's Peter Arnold circulating the high-speed bowl at Millbrook Proving Ground in Car 006. Circulating at 140mph while trying to see through the oncoming gloom is oddly boring and scary at the same time. The sensation of being at an angle becomes normal after 10 minutes. This RS200 went on to serve as a rally car and then became a parts donor for Car 072, which was owned by a Portuguese rally team.

RS ICONS EDITION  099

**Six of the first**
Limited – very limited – production of 194 RS200s started after this sixth and final car was made. The hard-working sextet were:
001 - First prototype, destroyed or repurposed as rally car
002 - Road car prototype used as crash test car
003 - Road car prototype B888 CHK
004 - Launch car at Turin show B690 CEV
005 - Rally car B55 CHK, won '85 Lindisfarne Rally
006 - Final road car prototype, converted to rally car B340 CAR

*Courtesy Peter Arnolt*

### Making it

Initial production ramped up slowly until Ford Motorsport deployed Bill Meade one of its experts at getting things done fast to speed things up. Cars were built using slave components where necessary, which allowed them to be finished offline. The temporary nature of the production line meant that staff from Reliant moved each car along on a wheeled dolly to the next production station: crude but effective.

*Courtesy Peter Arnolt*

*Courtesy Dave Boulton*

### End of the line

The production RS200s followed the six prototypes. Each of the 194 cars was hastily assembled over four months in late 1985. The rules for Group B included provision that the 200 units be made available for inspection by the FIA and a competitor. This was undertaken in January '86 although the 200 cars were by no means complete. Nonetheless, the sporting authorities were satisfied that Ford had created 200 separate cars, even though they were never seen together, and granted homologation. This picture, taken just after the FIA examination, shows that Car 200 certainly existed. Here, Tickford's Dave Boulton stands proudly beside it. How many were driveable at the time? "Well, I'd say around five!" says one of the Tickford team. It mattered not; the correct number of cars had been made, and Tickford was now charged with rebuilding the road cars for sale, although some were dismantled for spares. The RS200 remains the only dedicated RS car not based on a production Ford. Sadly, it never got its time in the sun: regulations changed and the far less specialised Sierra RS500 went on to fill Ford's medals cabinet. Wherever that is.

### Nine multiplied by...

RS200 prices start at around £200,000 today, but an ex-works car can cost double that. There are nine complete RS200s in this photo, making a cool £7-8 million in today's money. But when Group B was cancelled, Ford found that the RS200's market — rally teams — had no use for them. Cars were initially sold at a discount until Ford discovered it had the wrong strategy. It was better to repaint and luxuriously retrim them and raise the price.

This is Tickford's facility just outside Coventry. In the centre of the photo is Tickford's Dave Wood, the workshop manager who test drove nearly every Tickford Capri, RS200 and Sierra RS500 built in this former hat-making factory. By a bizarre twist of fate, around 20 per cent of Tickford staff were called Dave, but this was the Dave who drove hundreds of cars that today are worth millions.

*Courtesy Dave Boulton*

### RS200's track record

The RS200's Chief Engineer, John Wheeler looks back on the car's competition career, "The RS200 won many events and several Championships in Europe in '86, including the British Rally Championship, West European, Portuguese and the Belgian Championships. From '87 onwards, the FIA World Rally changed to Group A cars after Group B was no longer allowed so we had to swing all works effort onto the Sierra Cosworth at short notice. Nonetheless, that year, the RS200 won several rallycross championships and many other non-FIA rally events.

# THE 16 MILLION DOLLAR GAMBLE

In May 2017, the authoritative *MotorSport* Magazine counted the cars that won the most races over a three-year period, not including specialised racers like F1 cars and thus the all-conquering McLaren MP4/4, which dominated the 1988 season. The winner, in every sense, was the Sierra RS500. The magazine calculated that the RS Ford won an astonishing 84.6 per cent of the races it entered. Seven times, across three seasons, the RS500 locked out the top 10 race positions in the British Touring Car Championship. In Australia, it won the Bathurst 1000 in '88 and '89 after being disqualified in '87 on a technicality. Had it not been for that infraction, it would also have won the inaugural '87 World Touring Car Championship by winning four, instead of three, races. As *MotorSport* said, while answering its own question: "Has another car ever been so comprehensively dominant?"

So let's look into how the RS500 came about, since it's a story untold in its entirety. It gives us the best possible excuse to look at images of the prototypes and images that I think have mainly only been seen as small black and white photos. Those cars, and the people behind them, at Ford and Tickford, have waited decades to tell you their stories.

The Sierra RS Cosworth's single purpose was to win in Group A racing. Regulations demanded a minimum of 5000 road going versions – plus, if the manufacturer wished, an additional 10 per cent 'Evolution' models. Volvo was a strong competitor and read the rule book carefully. To homologate the 240 Turbo Evolution for the '84 season, Volvo needed to build 500 copies, but the rules didn't stipulate that they had to *sell* any of them. After the FIA's inspection, Volvo promptly removed each car's large turbo, water injection and the recalibrated fuel injection system – leaving buyers with an otherwise mechanically standard vehicle that retained just a large intercooler. The 240 Turbo Evolution came into its own the next year and, in the hands of the Swiss Eggenberger team, it won the '85 European Touring Car Championship for Volvo.

**Black and white**
This vehicle was the third of four prototypes Tickford used to develop the RS200. The first car, D112 VEV was built under the direction of John Griffiths at Ford Motorsport. These first cars were painted white so that Tickford could easily inspect the bodies for damage during testing and development work. Just as well: Car 001 was used so hard that the inner wing split, and it was re-shelled. Car 003 fared better: it was just afflicted by several hours of bug-splattering at 150mph. The next 10 cars were built in March '87 to production spec for use as press cars and for final testing. They were painted black because it absorbs heat and puts more thermal load on the vehicle.

*Courtesy Peter Arnold*

In 1986, Ford contracted Eggenberger to ditch the Swedes and run the new Merkur XR4Ti. It was a perfect test bed for the following season's '87 Sierra RS Cosworth and allowed Ford to determine exactly what parts would need to be added for the 500 Evolution models. Volvo's rule-bending had been controversial, and Lothar Pinske at Ford Motorsport in Cologne realised that Ford would need to build *and* sell these 500 race-bred specialist Sierra Cosworth road cars.

Eggenberger issued a wish-list of three things: extra aero downforce, a large-turbo engine capable of 450bhp in race trim and revised rear suspension points. After some careful rulebook reading, Pinske realised that although the 500 evolution vehicles needed to have all the extra race-spec items fitted as standard, there was no mandate that the components had to function on the road car! A wish-list was one thing, but delivering it was another matter.

*Courtesy Dave Boulton*

### Wax and wash

The 496 cars that passed through Tickford's Bedworth facility were initially jetwashed to remove the wax applied for their six months of storage at Dagenham. Tickford's workshop started out as a haberdashery factory before its owners spotted an opportunity stitching fabrics for the growing automotive industry nearby. The Coventry Hood & Seating Company became part of CHI Industrials, which part-owned Aston Martin. The site was used by its Tickford spin-off to make the first 250 Jaguar Cabriolets, the Tickford Capri and to fettle the RS200, RS500, and a car SVE rarely admitted to, the highly forgettable Orion 1600E.

Special Vehicle Engineering was flat out during '84/85 readying the Escort RS Turbo and then the regular Sierra RS Cosworth for production. So it didn't have spare capacity to engineer these 500 specialist cars. But that wasn't going to stop Motorsport boss Stuart Turner: he had just the right people in his own team. John Griffiths, Boreham's engine and homologation expert, was tasked with working with Cosworth on the road version of the 500-off engine which, in race trim, would be making around 500bhp. Since Cosworth was a race engine maker it was more than capable of designing at speed but the bigger issue was logistical. Motorsport's product planner, Mike Moreton, was tasked with getting an additional 500 base cars made for conversion to evo spec, along with special components like the aero kit that needed to be designed and manufactured. On top of that, the prototypes had to be tested and certified and a way found to build the 500 upgraded cars.

*Courtesy Shaun Skinner Tickford Owners Club*

### RS500 on the grid
Unconverted cars were driven in at the rear of Tickford's workshop, which was divided into five lines of four production stations in a five-by-four grid. This was the first station, where a technician balefully looks down at the dirt under the standard rear spoiler he has just removed, along with the front bumper. The RS500 rear spoiler was installed and these redundant parts sent back to Ford for retention as spare service parts.

**Open wide**
Bonnets were removed at the second station and stored alongside the car on its production journey to avoid mismatches. Each car now worked its way forward to the front of the grid.

**Ramping up**
After removing the bonnet and mechanicals at the second station, cars were hoisted high in the air for the rear suspension brackets to be added. They were no use on the road and served no function but their presence was essential for the racing fraternity. The lower rear spoiler came from the humble Sierra 2.0iS but with a cut-out for the support spar of the spoiler above.

*Courtesy Shaun Skinner Tickford Owners Club*

When Moreton started in July '86, he soon realised that time was not on his side. The British market was the only one large and enthusiastic enough to take 500 specialist Sierra Cosworths with 10 per cent more power but a 20 per cent higher retail price. At £19,950, the project was projected to make a modest profit of just under $1000 per car. But it was a massive risk that meant that Ford had to build and push into dealer stock $16 million worth of RS cars to make a modest 3.5 per cent profit. The small return would be justified if it won but wiped out if Ford had to support dealer margins with incentives. That was a real risk since the RS500's showroom success would inevitably be tied to how well the racing Cosworth performed on the track. It might also be a tough sell if the more expensive 500-off cars were seen as poor value, or dated-looking versus the facelifted Sierra that would be on sale at the same time. To mitigate that risk, Ford of Britain Marketing requested that the 500 evo cars be on sale by July '87 to avoid them looking hopelessly outdated. Most importantly of all, the 500 cars needed to be homologated ASAP to compete in the '87 race season. The clock was ticking and being late put $16 million at risk.

Five thousand Sierra Cosworths had been scheduled for manufacture at the end of the year, just before the new facelifted version started going down the line. Moreton's first task was to go to the very top, manufacturing boss Bill Hayden, and plead for the additional 500 to be added to the run. Hayden was noted for terrifying even finance people thanks to his extraordinary grasp of numbers and logistics, which meant he usually got what he wanted. Thankfully, he granted Moreton's wish and the extra cars were added to the build schedule for construction over a two-week period in December '86 and then put into storage at Dagenham while awaiting conversion the next year. Moving from logistics to execution, Griffiths and Moreton turned their attention to the Cosworth's 500 uprated engines which, like the rest of the body and chassis changes, needed to be designed, tested *and* meet all road-going homologation standards. The evolution car's simple and efficient aero kit was devised in the Cologne wind tunnel by Motorsport's Eberhardt Braun. Removing the fog lights and adding a front bumper slot increased the cooling. Extra downforce came from a deeper front spoiler lip and a flap on

*Courtesy Shaun Skinner Tickford Owners Club*

### Almost there
These were the last cars being assembled, here at the fourth station, where they were checked for quality. The car on the left has Tickford's trade plate tucked behind its windscreen so that it can head out to the nearby back roads where Tickford tested each car. The same eight-mile route was used for the Tickford Capri and RS200. Locals became blasé about seeing hundreds of Ford's most expensive '80s icons romping by each day.

the rear spoiler, with a second lower spoiler as seen in rudimentary form on RST10. The Sierra Cosworth's lead designer, Harm Lagaay, had left for BMW Technik and so the quick task of finalising the appearance for the RS500's new aero parts was done – "in an afternoon, as I recall" – by Luc Landuyt, who happened to be crafting the look of the four-door Sierra Cosworth at the same time.

Although Karmann had been considered as one solution to make the cars, Tickford was far better placed to production engineer and finish off the vehicles. It had engineers of proven ability who had taken the RS200 into limited production, and a facility outside Coventry that could modify the 500 cars. They would only be sold in Britain so Tickford's location reduced the job of shuttling them around Europe. In November '86, Tickford was appointed to handle the task of taking the Motorsport RS500 prototype from concept to production reality in just eight months. Former Tickford engineer Dave Boulton recalls: "The specification we received was well-defined, with packaging established and engine layout information available. Naturally, we had to make various production changes, such as replacing the

### An inspector calls

The official inspection by the FIA on July 13 1987 was conducted by Eberhardt Moor, the Federation's representative who had earlier signed off the RS200's homologation. This time it was easy: all 500 cars were parked together and ready for scrutiny. Moor was accompanied by ex-Ford competitions boss Thomas Ammerschläger, who had moved to BMW Motorsport in '85. Although approval was granted, the last of the 500 vehicles were not finished for another two weeks, at the end of July, and immediately shipped out mid-August.

*Courtesy Dave Boulton*

fabricated end tanks of the intercooler with aluminium castings because it was cheaper at that volume. The major work was productionising the engine installation with items such as an increased diameter air intake system, larger turbo, exhaust, and associated heat shields. Effectively, it was a total engine bay redraw."

After three months labour, while fitting the project in between others, Tickford had engineered the RS500 for production. By April '87 four prototypes completed Ford's test schedules for high-speed durability. They also endured the torture of Belgian pavé as they accumulated road mileage on the way to passing legally mandated drive-by noise and emission standards. Cosworth agreed to remanufacture the engines, which would be removed from the 500 donor cars. Now all Tickford had to do was complete testing and begin training 44 workshop staff to make an initial 10 training cars during March and April before the remaining RS500s were converted over a six-week period starting in mid-June.

**Trailer for what was around the corner**
Sales started immediately. The RS500 and the Sierra Cosworth that sired it were born out of troubled times at Ford in late '83 when the Sierra was struggling and the XR4i flagship missed the mark. So the RS500 could not have arrived at a better time than in late '87, as it did, and its winning ways were just around the corner... and on the straights. Statistics tell us it was the most successful racing car ever but the benefit to Ford's reputation at the time was priceless.

*Courtesy Dave Boulton*

# UNDERNEATH THE 4X4 ESCORT

If you ask Rod Mansfield, the former manager of SVE, what was his favourite car-that got-away, he will nominate this one. This is what crawling under the cancelled Escort 4x4 from 1986 looks like. It's one of 10 prototypes that followed the first white car seen here and on page 292 of *Secret Fords Volume One*. I had these photos sitting on my computer for years, but they were badly exposed and – let's be honest – not exactly as glamorous as design models or sexy sketches. Thankfully, modern digital tools came to the rescue and restored the images so that you can see the rear suspension and propshaft that lurked beneath the 4x4 Escort that never hit dealer showrooms. One evening while I was working at Ford, my friend Tim had this car out for appraisal and so we did what we probably should not have – hoisted it on a wobbly trolly jack while I took these photos. As I recall, the car wasn't all that special on the road. The mild fun of driving an XR3i with an RS *turbo* engine wasn't much to write home about when 50 per cent of the cars in Essex at the time were new Fords of some sort or another. The one that got away? Well, sometimes a secret Ford is OK remaining that way.

**Raising a glass too soon**
The Escort 4x4 was killed because of timing: the EFI engine planned for it ran late, which meant that by the time it came out volumes would have been too small. But not everything was wasted. Peer at the underside and one can just see the novel 'saddlebag' fuel tank either side of the rear differential. The idea was reused on the '90s next-generation AWD Escort RS2000.

*Courtesy Geoff Fox*

# THE END OF AN ICONIC ERA

The RS500 was developed by Motorsport at a time when SVE was busy simultaneously readying its successor, the four-door Sierra Cosworth. It turned out to be one of the most successful RS cars of all. These are the first two prototypes, up and running in August '86, months before the first RS500 prototype was even on the road — well, test track then. The late '80s are drawing in now and inevitably the conclusion of the journey for this companion book to *Secret Fords Volume One* beckons. But it's by no means the end because we have some fun ahead. If you have *Secret Fords Volume Two — RS Special Collector's Edition*, then you'll know that there is a whole host of '90s and 2000s cars waiting to tell their story. But one RS tale I didn't get to relate in that book is another Sierra one. I think it belongs in this

**Tyre testing**
The cones placed on the track by the SVE team at Goodyear's Mireval testing ground were set up to test brakes a little and steering feel and grip a lot. Magazines and TV lead us to think that test track work involves tailslides and high speeds but much of the time that's not how cars — even high-performance ones — are driven. This tight slalom test couldn't be conducted at high speed but provided something more valuable: what the car would be like during a 50mph swerve. The Mireval site includes extensive hosing to flood parts of the various tracks to allow controlled test comparisons with wet and dry situations on different road surfaces.

RS ICONS EDITION  113

**First of their kind**
The blue car wore a British B registration after starting life as a very early prototype. Following a year's-worth of work as a 1600cc car, it was converted in summer '86 to use Cosworth running gear. Ironically, red and mid-blue were two of the rarer colours used on the production cars and for that reason are highly sought-after today. Red suited the car well but was hardly subtle and had an all-too-obvious similarity to regular 1.6Ls driven by sales reps. These first two Cosworth saloons ended their days long before production versions hit the road.

*Courtesy Peter Hitchins*

book because of the long and glorious shadow that car, along with the Capri and Escort, casts over the RS saga. I'll tell it now and then hand you over to the bonus pages ahead that originally featured in this book's predecessor as part of the *Secret Fords Volume One Collector's Edition* two-book set. And, since we do have to say goodbye in the closing pages, I'll finish on a high with the jewels of the RS crown as we take a lingering look over each RS wheel from the '70s and '80s. The highs and lows of the RS brand in the '90s and 2000s lay ahead – but that story belongs to another period and is told in *Secret Fords Volume Two*. So let's close – for now – by dipping a toe in the '90s water with one of the most enigmatic and mysterious RS Sierras that few have ever heard of.

# THE *OTHER* SIERRA RS

Apartheid in South Africa lasted from the late '40s until the early '90s. Economic sanctions and political sensitivity meant that car manufacturers had to give greater autonomy to their local organisations to develop vehicles and powertrains for road and track. Ford South Africa created the V8 powered Sierra XR8 and 3.0litre Essex-engined XR6, but was not alone in conjuring up interesting mongrels. Alfa Romeo built a South Africa-only tuned-up GTV 3.0 V6 and since BMW could not sell the M3 in SA it teamed up with Alpina to make the 333i by stuffing the 733i engine into a 3 Series. These glorious road-going concoctions were, like the Sierra Cosworth, created for motorsport homologation but Ford South Africa's engineering abilities stretched beyond niche sporty cars. The Escort Bantam and Cortina P100 pickups, seen in *Secret Fords Volume One* are two examples and then there is this one – the *other* Sierra RS.

South Africa was nearing the end of apartheid in 1990 but Ford South Africa still couldn't import engines. So the wily locals continued to make the Essex V6 at their Struandale Engine Plant. Although the heavy old motor had been abandoned in Ford's European cars after the Capri Injection's debut nearly 10 years earlier, it had continued in the South Africa-only Sierra XR6. But car and engine were ageing, and the South Africans hatched a plan to make the V6 cleaner and increase its power in a two-stage process. In late '90, the compression ratio was pushed up to 9.5:1 to boost low-end torque. Free-flow heads, manifolds and a revised valvetrain, driven by a higher-lift camshaft that was less prone to high-speed bounce, let it rev higher. That first round of fiddling was no more than a warm-up for the more substantive addition a year later when Lucas fuel injection was added. Power leapt to 157bhp, more than the 150bhp quoted for the contemporary 2.9litre Cologne SOHC V6 used in the European Sierra and Scorpio.

The RHD South African five-door was marketed as Sierra and the four-door version as simply Sapphire – without the Sierra name. The Essex V6 had been principally used in the five-door XR6 but,

**Not what it seems at the front**
This RHD car wearing British plates looks like any contemporary Sierra Sapphire one might have seen in a Tesco's car park, but it's not. This is a UK-imported car, one of the 150 red and white Sapphire 3.0i RS cars from South Africa that sported special wheels and stripes to differentiate it from the five-door Sierra 3.0i RS that was built in unlimited numbers. Buyers could opt for the full-on Cosworth look and swap these rims for optional lattice-style wheels.

having invested in the upgraded motors, Ford SA elected to put it into the P100 pickup and the less sporty GLX and Ghias. The new range-topper to replace the five-door XR6 was the 3.0i RS, which looked identical to the European-market XR4x4 but with RWD and more power. OK; more power, but with a 0-100km/h time of 9.3 seconds it was hardly neck-snapping, thanks to heavy leather trim and the onset of age that added equipment and weight. It was no faster than the five-door-only XR6.

There was a marketing opportunity here: a numbered run of 150 red and white four-door 3.0i RS Sapphires that featured unique wheels, stripes, and the cachet of being (if one didn't look too closely) a visual doppelgänger of the Sierra Sapphire Cosworth. The Sierra story was finally ending, so it's appropriate that the last version, with a new engine, featured the same two RS letters that saved the car and cemented it as part of Ford's sporting legacy.

### Not Quite What It Says At The Rear

The badge says RS but here's the reality. Ford South Africa's print ads plastered the word RENNSPORT (German for motor racing) across the top. Ford used the RS letters, like Chevrolet, Audi and Porsche, on several machines on various high-performance products. Yes, back in the '80s there was a Mustang RS too, but did the letters make it a Rallye Sport car? The same applied here: yes, it's a Sierra RS but not a Rallye Sport car as we know them.

# BONUS PAGES

Fourteen of the following pages first appeared in the Scrapbook contained within *Secret Fords Volume One Collector's Edition*. With that edition out of print, I wanted them to be enjoyed here in its successor. They may not be RS cars, but they still have some fascinating secret stories to tell. As a bonus, I've added images that came into my hands since I wrote the Scrapbook. Enjoy them now: the '70s secret Fords are back, one last time.

### Genesis of Capri

Flowline was the British-designed alternative to the American GBX, the car that became Capri. I included a side shot of Flowline in The Cars You Always Promised Yourself but it has never been glimpsed from the front or rear before. These two photos, shot in January 1965, and the rendering turned up too late for my two Capri-centric books but not for this scrapbook, so here they are. Flowline, the Capri you never promised yourself, was a Capri but not as we know it. You be the judge of which would have made a better production car.

RS ICONS EDITION  117

**A new angle on the first Capri**
This photo remained hidden for more than 50 years. It was worth the wait: it's the only picture of the original American-designed GBX in the UK. The angle is unusual too. It shows us something never seen before: GBX had fire-breathing nostrils in its bonnet. It is far longer than the production Capri that followed; the Brits had to shrink the American concept for production. I can't imagine I'll ever write another Capri book, so here it is.

*Courtesy Steve Aylen*

# GRANADA GHIA NUMBER ONE

I can't claim to have been a fan of the original Granada Ghia. By the time I got to Ford they were all a little too dog-eared and tired-looking compared to Patrick le Quément's crisp-looking '77 Eva model. But when they were new... well, that's a different story. This is the sign-off model for the Granada Ghia. As you'd expect, it has tiny differences in wheels and badging from the production car. But that's not what caught my eye. Who was the genius who put a silver/grey vinyl roof on a silver car? It adds a sense of class and style that works perfectly with the circular Ghia badge nestling into it. Ghia loved embedding its crest within vinyl-covered pillars, yet I can't think of a single production Ford that followed suit.

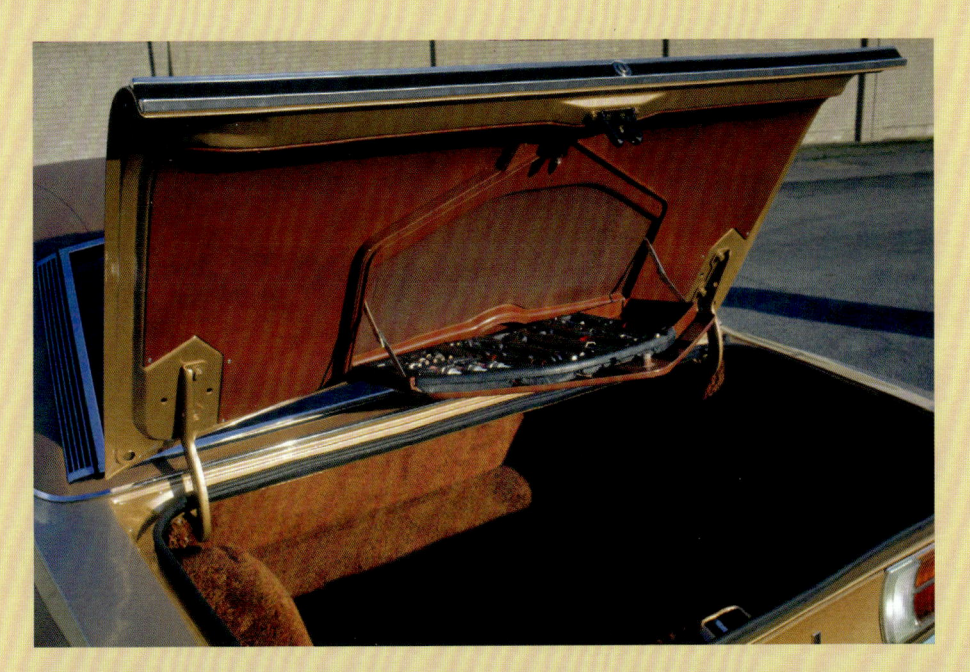

**Browned to perfection**
This almost needs no caption. I have no idea who designed this Granada interior. Despite the badge, the photos didn't come from the Ghia archive; they are discarded Dunton pictures. Thank heavens Andy Plumb picked them up when they were thrown out. It's an astonishing interior, especially when you consider it's from an era of stick-on vinyl wood. It seems so much sportier and more expensive. There are lots of exterior designs in this book that one might wonder about, but not this interior. It's in a different league from the production Granada and proves how good Dunton's interior designers were. I can't avoid looking at the dashboard and thinking about the rocker switches in a '70s Jaguar XJ6 — and that toolkit!

# STANDING ON EDOUARD'S SHOULDERS

When I was a teenager, an excellent book by Edouard Seidler titled *Let's Call It Fiesta* inspired me to work for Ford. It also inspired two of my friends who worked at BMW. The French author wrote in his intro: "This [book] is only the history of its birth. One day, perhaps, someone will write its life story." As I wrote *Secret Fords'* Bobcat chapter, I felt that I needed to do Seidler proud and stand on the shoulders of his work. It's for others to judge whether I succeeded, but I could not believe the amount of Fiesta material I was able to unearth, from the incredible shots of the seating bucks inside the Dunton design showroom though to buried treasures like this series from the Ghia archive.

**Baby blue**
The Bobcat Fiesta was heavily influenced by Ghia and, in particular, the work of Tom Tjaarda. His first concept was the so-called 'Blue Car'. These low-res images are the only colour ones I could find. Ford found a two-door Blue Car in the Ghia archive, which I included in the book, along with a black and white shot, but not these.

**Problem children**
This set of photos illustrates the problem that the product planners faced with the B-Car project. The Americans (back then) wanted station wagons and four-door sedans while the Europeans were rushing towards hatchbacks. This is the station wagon/estate version of the Fiesta Bobcat seen on Page 79. Although Henry Ford II wanted the Fiesta to sell in the US, the cards were stacked against it. When petrol prices dropped in 1977, so did sales. The same thing happened to the stateside Fiesta (and Focus) in the late 2010s. A small fuel-efficient hatchback just doesn't appeal to Americans.

RS ICONS EDITION  **121**

**Two teams, many fathers, one Fiesta**
I had seen images of these two cars in Edouard Seidler's book and they fascinated me – the two competing British and German submissions for the Fiesta. The Dunton design, created under the leadership of Jack Telnack, wears '000 000' plates. Uwe Bahnsen's German-based team created the other car, identified using the customary 'K-LN-000' plate seen on many of these pages. The British car is the direct descendant of Tom Tjaarda's Blue Car and the later Wolf, while the Germans struck out on their own path. From this angle it's clear to see – for the first time – that the Cologne team won out from the front but, as Jack reminded me, the British design had greater influence on the rear. That's the way design goes: a bit of this added to bit of that from another theme. There's a lot written about who designed the Fiesta: it certainly wasn't Tom Tjaarda or Jack Telnack or Uwe Bahnsen, but a team.

122  Secret Fords

*Courtesy Andy Plumb*

## STEP INSIDE

**Take a seat, have a look**
I could look at these all day. Andy Plumb sent a huge haul of Bobcat interior shots from 1975 showing the Base, L and Ghia seating bucks. The main picture is especially atmospheric. I remember even now walking into the Dunton design showroom for the first time. The blue Ghia interior was a design marvel and deserved to win the awards given to it.

**RS ICONS EDITION** **123**

**A little bit of heart and soul**
I loved the style of this rendering by Brian Hughes and used it as a tiny thumbnail in my first Ford book *The Cars You Always Promised Yourself*. But it really deserved more space and so here it is to enjoy. This painstakingly drawn piece was created after the Fiesta Ghia interior was finished and one can almost touch the (plastic) wood and touch that buzz-cropped velour fabric. On occasions, car designers will say sniffily of another's work "Well they are more of an illustrator than a designer" to signify the difference between their own self-proclaimed creative genius versus a lesser mortal who is merely able to draw. They may be right; this rendering is more than just a visual record; it captures the very heart and soul of the Fiesta Ghia perfectly.

# MYSTERIOUS MONICA

This one didn't make the book but it has an interesting tale. Project Monica was a slightly upmarket FWD saloon developed by Ghia during 1974. The intention was to add something European to the US Ford range that could be sold against the compact premium cars that were beginning to make headway in the US, ironically with RWD. Ford was slow in moving towards FWD but research showed that buyers preferred it until you got into the premium market. So why did Ghia develop these cars and why was this car FWD? The first question is easily answered by these black and white photos. The De Tomaso Deauville four-door and Longchamp coupe were designed by Tom Tjaarda at Ghia, just before Ford bought the studio. Monica bears a striking resemblance to a shrunken two-door Longchamp. No need to ask who designed her at Ghia then... The second question — why FWD — is connected to the eternal struggle that some factions inside Ford had with creating a minivan/MPV. Lee Iacocca was convinced that the minivan was the next big thing. He was right: minivans eventually took 20 per cent of the market. But a minivan needed a C-segment FWD platform and Ford didn't have one. This was Iacocca's plan: sneak a FWD platform in under Project Monica, an upmarket saloon, and build the Minivan he wanted. Henry Ford II was beginning to mistrust Iacocca and didn't like the idea of a minivan, so he killed the project. He had just funded the Erika Escort and had no wish to make an investment in something as risky as Monica.

RS ICONS EDITION  125

# THE SECRET SOCIETY OF GRANADAS

It's difficult to describe how much my head spun when I saw all these different iterations of Granada. It rotated even faster when the Granada's designer, Patrick le Quément, professed that even he hadn't seen many of them, such as the adorable Model D that pays homage to BMW's Six. Go ahead; pick your favourite. Mine's bottom left.

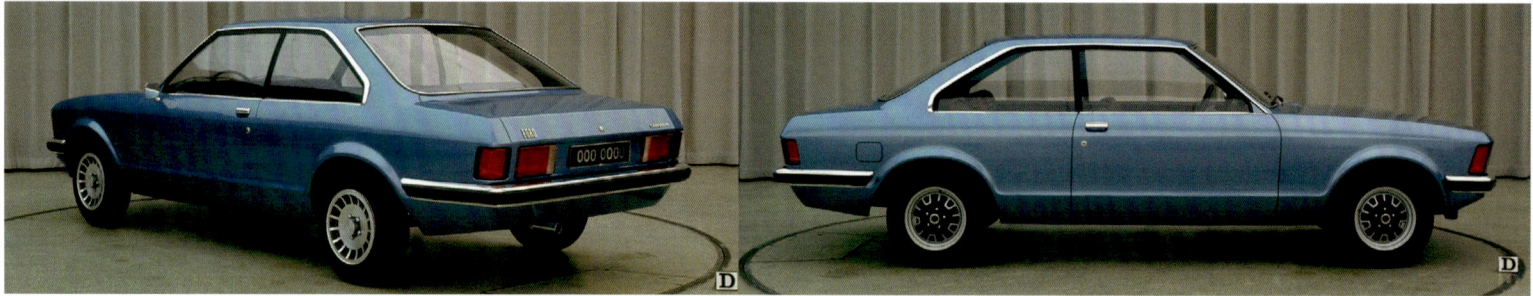

**RS ICONS EDITION** 127

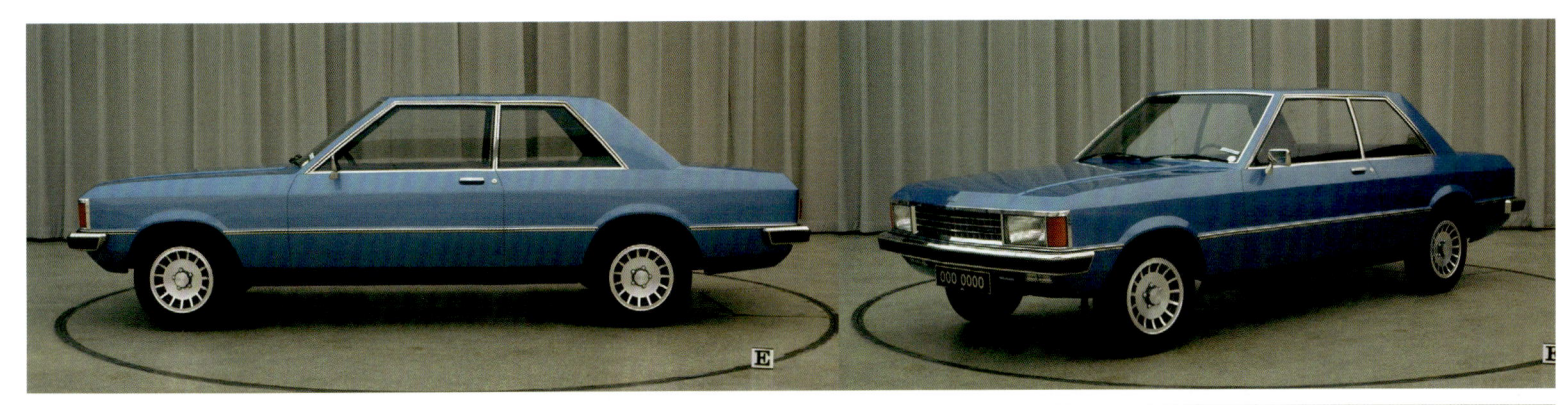

*Courtesy Andy Plumb*

# THE CAPRIS WE NEVER PROMISED OURSELVES

### Take a seat
These Capri Ghia seat drawings were created by Dunton designer Graham Symonds who just happened to be an Olympic swimmer in his spare time. There's nothing watered-down about these wonderful sketches which show how the novel folding seats worked. Every SUV might have them as standard today but the Capri was one of the first.

### Ghia's added gear
The Ghia badge might have been relegated to a trim level early on in its life but that doesn't mean that the Ghia designers didn't offer Merkenich their opinion. This picture is fascinating: found buried deep inside Ghia's archives, it shows the Italians' take on a Capri Ghia. It's an odd but simple modification job shot with lots of unusual detail. A bodyside moulding runs down around the wheelarch, just as on the original '69 car. Like so many of the concept studies seen in *Secret Fords*, there's a padded B-pillar bearing the Ghia crest, and a none-too subtle chrome wheelarch trim. At a guess, it's likely that this vehicle was created after Capri production started – it's certainly a real car and not a fibreglass mockup. The Capri Ghia's interior might have been designed in Essex, but Ghia still offered up ideas for the exterior of the car bearing its name.

# CAPRI 2.8 INJECTION

**Laser Injection**
Dunton's Design courtyard sometime in late '82. This is the Laser prototype surrounded by Sierra doors in the distance painted in new, unseen colours. This Laser had a 2.8litre V6 and Recaro seats, unlike production cars that were saddled with just four cylinders and humdrum seating.

**The Ford giveth and the Ford taketh away**
As the Capri got older, Ford needed to keep the interior fresh – it was much loved. The problem was that the four-cylinder cars had been given expensive Recaro seats; what more could the product planners do? This was the car used to get to the solution. Give the new Laser model the expensive Injection trim pack but swap in some cheapo Escort GL seats. That's the product planners' juggling act: give buyers something extra here and take away something else there.

**Say "i" for Injection**
That would have been a happy way to spend the afternoon. Everyone loves playing with badge designs, especially on a sporty car like the Capri. This was how they did it in the old days – using bits of paper. The Capri Injection might have been badged plain-old 2.8i or, a little later the 2.8 Laser.

*Courtesy Steve Aylen*

# THE FIRST TC2, SIXTH-GENERATION TAUNUS, CORTINA MARK IV

### Codebreaker

There are lots of first-this-and-that design models in *Secret Fords*. This is the first Taunus/Cortina. Note the racy door mirrors, non-standard taillights and the FORD TAUNUS badges. To Brits, it was the Mark IV Cortina but to Ford insiders it was TC2. Why TC2? Simple really: the Taunus had lived through four generations — confusingly, in two sizes — until 1970. The larger version was replaced by the Granada and the smaller by the 1970 TC, the first Taunus/Cortina which Brits knew as the Cortina Mark III and Germans the Sixth Generation Taunus. So, time to reset the codenaming committee's clock, and TC it was. This second-generation car became the TC2 and its successor, the 1980-model facelift, was often internally dubbed TC3. But because the naming committee was always hard at work, and deep into girl's names, it was officially codenamed Project Teresa. *An Introductory Guide To Ford Codenames* is a small and very complex book that I shall never write.

*Courtesy Andy Plumb*

# REINVENTING THE WHEEL

From their earliest days, RS cars have featured distinctive wheels. Like badges, seats, colour and trim, they have always been as much at the heart of the brand as a tuned engine and chassis. I covered the evolution of the RS logo design in the three-book set *Secret Fords Volume Two RS Collector's Edition*, which featured almost every wheel on its cover. But there wasn't the space to examine the wheels in that book so this is the perfect opportunity to take a long last look as the two Volumes shake hands, and I say goodbye. The first RS wheels fitted to the 15M, 17M and 20M cars of the '60s were simple steel items garnished with chrome and black paint, but in the decades ahead Ford got into the swing of reinventing the wheel with ever more extravagant alloy designs. So let's go back to the late '60s with a 20-year review of what kept the RS brand rolling forward.

## The first RS wheel

The first RS wheel was — like so many of its successors — unique to the RS models that it was fitted to. The smaller 15M RS used a skinny 4½-inch width with a relatively tall 14-inch diameter, while the larger 17M/20M RS cars used the same wheel in a ½-inch wider, 5-inch width. Although the first two RS cars came with radial ply tyres as standard, the regular 15M and 17M/20M still used cross ply tyres; the '60s were an era long before road-hugging wide, low-profile tyres became a hallmark of high-performance vehicles. Contemporary Ford wheels used hubcaps, but the first RS rims adopted a unique look that reimagined the much-admired matte dark grey- and silver-painted British Rostyle wheels. In a bit of Cologne one-upmanship over the Brits, the pioneering RS wheel deployed a chrome finish with a satin-black centre and a five-stud fitment. The result was a tasteful, unique, and distinctive look that set the style template for the decades of RS wheels that followed.

## Minilite

In the early 1960s, after Henry Ford II changed his mind about motorsport and Total Performance became the company's mantra, Ford might have been 100 per cent committed to racing — but winning wasn't plain sailing. Success was hard-won, especially in rallying where the BMC Mini was formidable thanks to a highly tuned engine that gave it speed, and light components that removed weight and added agility. One of the Mini's secrets was a specially designed competition wheel made of expensive magnesium, which was volatile when machined on a lathe but ultra-light when finished. Designed in 1962 by the wonderfully named John Ford and Derek Power, this new wheel improved the Mini's handling and performance. It had another advantage: Ford and Power's design used aerodynamic theory to sweep air over the little Mini's brakes. Not only did the wheels help it accelerate and corner better, but the little car stopped faster too. Designing and making the wheel might have been difficult but naming it was easy — Minilite. Other racers took note and it was only a matter of time before car manufacturers realised this new wheel could improve any car: Ford was one of the first and fitted it to the first lightweight Capri RS2600s and offered it as an option on the first-generation AVO Escorts.

## M.A.G

The Mini's success led to a host of related companies that created aftermarket accessories for anybody wanting to go — or at least look — a bit faster. One involved rally driver Paddy Hopkirk, who lent his name to a range of go-faster goodies. No doubt he made more money from them than the mediocre fees paid to drivers back in the '70s. The Paddy Hopkirk business grew enough that it was absorbed with others into one entity called Mill Accessory Group (M.A.G) which also supplied the eponymously named Richard Grant Accessories, which specialised in wheels, seats and spoilers. M.A.G. developed a range of aftermarket alloy wheels of varying styles that it supplied to vehicle manufacturers as well as the aftermarket. Although its rims were aluminium alloy, 'MAG wheels' had — thanks to a clever play on three letters — the same verbal cachet as the more expensive magnesium Minilite jobs. Cost was always close to Ford's heart and after the first run of 50 lightweight Capri RS2600 cars, production switched to these M.A.G. items. They were unusual and attractive but were not fitted to the production Capri RS2600 for long, and the bumperless car switched back to Minilites.

## AVO Escort Styled Steel Sports Wheel

The Escort Twin Cam and Mexico used plain hubcaps and it wasn't until the RS2000 that Ford designers upped their game for the Escort. They crafted the clumsily-named Styled Steel Sports Wheel as an elegant — well, elegantly cheap — way of adding alloy wheel style at a steely-eyed low price thanks to grey paint and a deeper offset. Although many chose to fit the classic RS Four-spoke, the alloy rim remained an option on most RS Escorts. Indeed, the Styled Steel Sports Wheel was standard fare on the second generation Escort Mexico, RS1800 and RS2000. But their popularity was too great to ignore, and different-sized versions soon found themselves on mainstream GL-spec Cortinas, Capris and Granadas. Pity the poor RS1800 owner who strove for originality only to find passing classic car show visitors commenting that the basic-looking, blue striped white car had 'Cortina wheels'.

## FAVO: AVO's four-spoke

The Le Mans-winning GT40 was based on a Lola race car, designed with input from Len Bailey. The former Ford engineer started working freelance and received another contract from his former employer, this time to design a rally car to a brief from Motorsport supremo Stuart Turner. Bailey, like so many engineers, fancied himself as much as a designer as an engineer. But, unlike many another aspiring Isambard Kingdom Brunel, he did possess design talent. The first show car was unveiled with four-spoke alloys so striking that they were called out in Ford's publicity. The new wheel was as strong as it looked, and the large gaps between the four spokes admitted cooling air for the brakes. For many, though, it was more about the style than the function — they looked special, as exotic and elegant as anything on a contemporary Italian sports car. Distinctive and made of aluminium alloy, the wheel was initially dubbed the FAVO wheel by Ford's Advanced Vehicle Operations (AVO) employees, but colloquially termed the RS alloy wheel. It became *the* RS wheel for many, going on to live an astonishingly long life after replacing the Minilite on the Capri RS2600. It soon found its way onto AVO's other premium car, the RS2000 Mark I and then the limited-run Capri II GT S, known by many as the JPS. Despite wheels being a fashion item, the design kept its appeal, and, in modified form, was carried over on to the beak-nosed RS2000 that Tom Scott designed. As the *Ford Rallye Sport Accessories* catalogue expanded, Ronal continued making the wheel well into the '80s as part of an ever-widening range of different sized wheel options. Now, owners of a Fiesta, FWD Escort, Capri Mark III, Cortina, and even the Granada, could sprinkle RS fairy dust onto their Fords. It wasn't just wannabe RS owners. Other production cars picked up the four-spoke wheel: Fiesta Supersport, Cortina XR6, Escort Harrier and Capri S all wore them too. But time was moving on and the last production RS to use the wheel was the LHD Capri *turbo* of 1981. The iconic four-spoke RS alloy became the longest-lived Ford wheel design: it arrived in 1972 and finally bowed out 15 years later on the 1987 Capri Laser. Five years is an exceptionally long time for any wheel to stay in production but 15 may be unique. If only Len Bailey had negotiated a royalty.

### Escort Mark 1 RS2000
Standard fit on some RS2000s and seen on countless other Escorts. For a while it was called the FAVO wheel after Ford Advanced Vehicle Operations but for many it remains *the* classic RS wheel.

### Capri RS2600, RS3100
Slightly more elegant than those found on the contemporary Escort, this version of the RS wheel is one of the hardest to find.

### Escort Mark 2 RS2000
The wheel was standard on the initial type of second-generation RS2000s and subsequent ones made with the Custom pack. The later versions had these dove grey painted centres, instead of the body colour that Tom Scott envisaged.

### Capri *turbo*
This 7½-inch wheel looks face-on just like the RS2000 wheel. But only the limited-run Capri *turbo* had it as standard — and even then, at a push. German rules dictated snow chains should be possible, so in theory, but not practice, it was an option.

## Seven-Spoke

Although the Escort RS1600i was a quickly-developed homologation special it sold extraordinarily well, in part because of its striking seven-spoke wheels. They were created at the request of Ford Motorsport's Thomas Ammerschläger before he moved to BMW. Ford needed a new RS wheel for the '80s that was easier to clean than the old four-spoke. Designers tend to like odd numbers of spokes; that's why five, seven or nine are common. Thomas Plath created a seven-spoke wheel with an unusual style that bowed outwards across its 15inch face, almost flaunting the offset needed for FWD, then a high-tech feature worth bragging about. Plath recalls his inspiration:

"I had seen a Porsche 928 design with a flat face that went right to the edge of the rim. It was expensive to cast but looked fantastic." Although Plath conceived the RS1700T with Ferrari-like five-spoke wheels, it was inevitable that his RS1600i wheel design was adopted for his rally car. The RWD car used a more complex-looking eight-spoke style that added strength but lacked the dished face of Plath's seven-spoke original. When the RS1600i handed over to the Escort RS Turbo, the wheel, with a few modifications, featured one last time on an RS model, the RS200 – in a bolted-together, split-rim 16-inch version that made wheel aficionados go

weak at the knees. Ford wasn't shy about using this new wheel design on non-RS cars, just as it had with the previous four-spoke design. Over time, it was fitted to the Scorpio 4x4, Capri Injection Special/280, XR4x4 and even the odd Orion Injection special edition. The RS Parts people got in on the act again too, quickly commissioning the wheel in various sizes for the Fiesta, Escort, Sierra, Capri and Scorpio, and the ultra-rare Sierra XR8. The seven-spoke RS wheel became just as iconic as its four-spoke predecessor but stayed in production for less time — just eight years — and finally rolled off the line on the last 1991 model Sierra 3.0i RS.

### Escort RS1600i, RS turbo

Although there were minor differences between the RS1600i and RS turbo wheels, they looked identical to anyone except the most ardent RS enthusiast. The flat face helped the wheels look bigger at a time when 14-inch diameter was considered large.

### RS200

The Escort RS1700T was intended to use this wheel in eight-spoke form. It was just too good to ignore for its successor, the RS200. A bolted-together split-rim version was available, which upped the ante in the wheel glamour

## Cosworth Cross-spoke

Dutch designer Harm Lagaay was tasked with making the Sierra Cosworth look acceptable. The first aero test car, based on an XR4i, was functional but not pretty. Harm's job was to fix that. When it entered Ford's Cologne wind tunnel in late 1983, the XR4i-based mule had 15-inch seven-spoke RS wheels, quickly made by Ronal which hoped they would be commissioned for production cars. Small batches of prototype wheels can be cast speedily in sand and machined at speed, but it was not to be. Instead, Lagaay abandoned the popular seven-spoke RS wheel for his masterpiece, the Sierra RS Cosworth.

The fastest Sierra had one job: to win races and burnish the car's tarnished reputation. Lagaay was a motorsport enthusiast and knew that racers would probably use BBS cross-spoke, split-rim wheels. He figured that, rather than use the seven-spoke RS design, he would imitate the BBS-look on the road car. His thinking was brilliant: the greater the similarity between the Sierra Cosworth road and race cars, the more owners would feel a connection between the two. When the RS500 began to win, appearing in magazines and on posters everywhere, it was clear: road and race cars were the same because... well, they looked the same.

## Lattice Wheel

Mainstream production cars in the late '80s began to include technology like ABS, 16-valve engines and fuel injection. Performance cars' style and performance needed to stay ahead. Tastes were changing and performance car buyers wanted more sophistication than a big turbo. All-wheel drive (AWD) was still called 4x4 — until the marketers realised it had too many off-road connotations. Ford planned to keep the Escort XR/RS twins, and Sierra RS, up to date by adding 4x4 and more sophisticated looks. French designer Luc Landuyt initially drew his Sierra Sapphire renderings with a variety of wheel options, from the swirled-spoke style of the Escort *turbo* through to split rims. But it was all speculative. As the second-generation Sierra Cosworth evolved, it needed to look more sophisticated and have appropriately discreet wheels. The result was a fantastically complex 20-spoke design with 10 spokes, arranged in pairs, overlaid on an identical set, and then rotated. Although the wheel was as difficult to describe as it was to clean, it helped define this more sophisticated ultimate Sierra — even if it did stray on to the less-than-sporty Argentine Sierra Ghia SX. Shortly after the Escort XR3i 4x4 was cancelled, the regular 1987 model adopted the same wheel in a smaller 14-inch size. One can assume that the two 4x4 Fords would have used a common wheel design had the Escort 4x4 made production. It wasn't the first and wouldn't be the last time that RS, XR and even Ghia models would share the same wheel style.

## '86 Escort RS *turbo*

The facelifted 1986 Escort was designed in 1984, just as the hot hatch was beginning to dominate the affordable performance car market. The hugely profitable XR2 made up 20 per cent of the Fiesta mix and the Escort XR3i wasn't far behind. Ford reasoned that if the second-generation RS Turbo was a little more refined then two sporty Escorts could make a significantly greater contribution. The problem for the design team was that the XR was the volume car that needed all the fashionable body-kitted aero addenda. But doing so would reduce the visual distinctiveness of the Escort RS *turbo* (now spelled out in italics). The solution was to design two similar-looking, five-spoke wheels — straight on the XR3i and swirled on the RS *turbo*. The XR was punished for its lesser rank with an unpainted black version of the rear spoiler that was body colour-matched on the RS. The idea worked. Well, sort of: it was almost impossible, unless you had trainspotter-like skills, to pick a black RS from a regular XR. The colour started being avoided by RS *turbo* buyers, who rushed to buy it in Mercury Grey or Rosso Red, two colours that worked especially well on the Escort. Making the RS and XR wheels look so similar was a rare design slip-up.

# INDEX

## DESIGNERS
**Bahnsen, Uwe** 80, 96, 121
**Callum, Ian** 26, 96
**Gotschke, Wolfgang** 70, 72
**Hartnell, John** 96
**Hatayama, Ichiro** 80, 82
**Jacobson, Andy** 96
**Jara, Tom** 72
**Lagaay, Harm** 80, 83, 86, 109, 134
**Landuyt, Luc** 109, 135
**Le Quément, Patrick** 32, 43, 80, 118, 126
**Nottrodt, Karl-Heinz** 26, 51
**Oros, Joe** 21, 24
**Plath, Thomas** 58, 62, 69, 71, 135
**Sapino, Filippo** 92
**Scott, Tom** 24, 30, 32, 34, 133
**Telnack, Jack** 33, 121
**Tjaarda, Tom** 120, 124

## DRIVERS
**Arikkala, Pentti** 59, 62
**Clark, Roger** 19, 37, 66
**Vatanen, Ari** 37, 66

## FORD DIVISIONS & DEPARTMENTS
**Competitions** 18, 109
**Design** 6, 38, 44, 88
**Motorsport** 3, 24, 26, 44, 46, 53-57, 61, 68, 78, 90, 92, 100, 104, 108, 112
**Special Vehicle Engineering** 4, 49, 51, 55, 67, 72, 78, 80, 84, 90, 97, 104, 111, 112

## FORD LOCATIONS
**Dagenham** 104
**Dearborn, Detroit** 24, 33, 76
**Dunton** 32, 44, 49, 80, 89, 96, 119, 120-121, 122, 129
**Lommel** 40
**Merkenich, Cologne** 6, 8, 80, 84, 94, 128

## FORD MANAGERS
**Ford, Henry,** *HFII* 39, 42, 120, 124, 131
**Fox, Geoff** 72
**Griffiths, John** 62, 103, 105, 108
**Hartwig, Gerhard** 42
**Lutz, Bob** 42, 44, 70, 74
**Mansfield, Rod** 20, 111
**Moreton, Mike** 92, 105, 107-108
**Turner, Stuart** 90, 105, 133
**Wheeler, John** 58, 92

## FORD VEHICLES
**'69 Capri 'Colt'** 17, 18-21, 116-117, 128-129
**'74 Capri 'Diana' and 'Carla'** 5, 10, 26-29, 45, 50-51, 52-57
**'75 Escort 'Brenda'** 30-35, 52,
**'81 Escort Erika** 38-39, 60-63, 90-91
**'81 Sierra 'Toni'** 7, 9, 40, 42-43, 68-73, 74-75, 76-89, 102-110
**'86 Escort** 111
**'87 Sierra** 112-113, 114-115
**15M, 17M, 20M** 12-15
**Fiesta 'Bobcat'** 36-37, 44, 120-124
**Granada** 6, 118-119, 126-127
**GT70** 22-28
**Merkur XR4Ti** 70-71
**RS200** 92-101